The Modern State Subverted

Risk and the Deconstruction of Solidarity

Giuseppe Di Palma

Cover Image: Fernand Léger, 'The Big Black Divers'
© 2013 Artists Rights Society (ARS), New York, ADAGP, Paris

First published by the ECPR Press in 2014

The ECPR Press is the publishing imprint of the European Consortium for Political Research
(ECPR), a scholarly association, which supports and encourages the training, research and
cross-national co-operation of political scientists in institutions throughout Europe and beyond.

ECPR Press
University of Essex
Wivenhoe Park
Colchester
CO4 3SQ
UK

Typeset by ECPR Press

Printed and bound by Lightning Source

Biitish Library Cataloguing in Publication Data

A catalogue record for this book is available from the Britlsh Library

ISBN: 978-1-907-301-63-6

www.ecpr.eu/ecprpress

ECPR Essays:

From Deliberation to Demonstration: Political Rallies in France, 1868–1939 (ISBN: 9781907301469) Paula Cossart

Hans Kelsen and the Case for Democracy (ISBN: 9781907301247) Sandrine Baume

Is Democracy a Lost Cause? Paradoxes of an Imperfect Invention
(ISBN: 9781907301247) Alfio Mastropaolo

Just Democracy (ISBN: 9781907301148) Philippe Van Parijs

Maestri of Political Science (ISBN: 9781907301193) Donatella Campus,
Gianfranco Pasquino, and Martin Bull

Masters of Political Science (ISBN: 9780955820335) Donatella Campus, and
Gianfranco Pasquino

ECPR Classics:

Beyond the Nation State: (ISBN: 9780955248870) Ernst Haas

Citizens, Elections, Parties: Approaches to the Comparative Study of the Processes of Development (ISBN: 9780955248887) Stein Rokkan

Comparative Politics: The Problem of Equivalence (ISBN: 9781907301414) Jan Van Deth

Democracy: Political Finance and state Funding for Parties (ISBN: 9780955248801)
Jack Lively

Electoral Change: Responses to Evolving Social and Attitudinal Structures in Western Countries (ISBN: 9780955820311) Mark Franklin, Thomas Mackie, and Henry Valen

Elite and Specialized Interviewing (ISBN: 9780954796679) Lewis Anthony Dexter

Identity, Competition and Electoral Availability: The Stabilisation of European Electorates 1885–1985 (ISBN: 9780955248832) Peter Mair and Stefano Bartolini

Individualism (ISBN: 9780954796662) Steven Lukes

Modern Social Policies in Britain and Sweden: From Relief to Income Maintenance (ISBN: 9781907301001) Hugh Heclo

Parties and Party Systems: A Framework for Analysis (ISBN: 9780954796617)
Giovanni Sartori

Party Identification and Beyond: Representations of Voting and Party Competition (ISBN: 9780955820342) Ian Budge, Ivor Crewe, and Dennis Farlie

People, States and Fear: An Agenda for International Security Studies in the Post-Cold War Era (ISBN: 9780955248818) Barry Buzan

Political Elites: (ISBN: 9780954796600) Geraint Parry

State Formation, Parties and Democracy (ISBN: 9781907301179) Hans Daalder

Territory and Power in the UK: (ISBN: 9780955248863) James Bulpitt

The State Tradition in Western Europe: A Study of an Idea and Institution (ISBN: 9780955820359) Kenneth Dyson

Please visit www.ecpr.eu/ecprpress for up-to-date information about new publications.

Contents

Acknowledgements

The story of this book is quickly told. In September 2008, I presented a paper at the annual meeting of the Italian Society of Political Science (SISP), held that year at the University of Pavia. The topic I was invited to deal with was the quality of democracy and its theories; the topic I ended up by dealing with was, in rudimentary form, the quality of democracy before and under neoliberalism. The paper was unfinished, yet already too long for a journal article. A number of colleagues urged me to make it into a book. The paper was in Italian. I decided, as a matter of pride, to write the book in Italian. Variously instrumental in offering precious comments as the volume took shape and in promoting its publication were Marco Almagisti (University of Padova), who had invited me to the Pavia meeting, Paolo Ceri (University of Florence), the late Giorgio Fedel (University of Pavia), Michele Salvati (University of Milano). Last but not least, there was Gianfranco Poggi, who at the time had closed his distinguished international career at the University of Trento. Gianfranco and I had been students together first at Padova, our *alma mater*, and then at Berkeley and had since remained friends and colleagues, increasingly in contact as we moved toward retirement. Gian was, unsurprisingly for the many who know him, an unstoppable force of nature in promoting publication of the finished book. The book was published by Rubbettino in April 2011 (*Viaggio nelle modernità. Rischio sociale e solidarietà dall'assolutismo al neoliberalismo*). A year later, Alfio Mastropaolo (University of Turin), read the book. We knew about each other but we had never met or corresponded. We initiated an ongoing correspondence *tous azimuts*, which I value as a cherished addition to my life after retirement. Unsolicited, Mastropaolo brought the book to the attention of ECPR Press.

A plain translation of the book was out of the question. In the first place, when I finished the volume for Rubbettino I already knew how I could improve it, if only I had the opportunity to refocus and rewrite. Writing is continuous learning. In the second place, to translate from Italian into English is to discover the enticing siren-like quality of my native language. An English sentence rendered verbatim into Italian sounds pedestrian, but a never-ending convoluted Italian sentence – of the type in which I nostalgically indulge – rendered verbatim in English reveals why the first ambassadors of early modernity spoke Italian. Thus, the present volume accomplishes three objectives. First, it lifts the veil of ambiguity under which some of my analysis, aided by my Italian, had taken cover. Second, having removed unpersuasive parts of the original, it introduces considerable new material, empirical and analytical, intended to strengthen and better focus what is left of the original. Third, it introduces new topics – on justice, criminalisation, and the management of new risks - intended to document in particular the extent to which neoliberalism, contrary to its claims of returning government to the people, micromanages and disciplines individual behaviour.

I close with a note of thanks to our daughter Vittoria. When it came to addressing the rise of discipline in the modern state, Vittoria suggested pairing Max Weber with Michel Foucault. It would have rounded, she argued, my argument that, under modernity, discipline is not just imposed but inscribed in each one of us. She proved convincing. Foucault's analysis of modern conduct as discipline is the object of attention throughout the book.

Giuseppe Di Palma,
November 2013

To Francine, a life together

Seek simplicity and distrust it

Alfred North Whitehead
mathematician, philosopher

Chapter One

The State and Civil Society: Revisiting the Past, Assessing the Present

From absolutism to liberalism and from liberalism to mass democracy, the modern Western state has been characterised by a special relation of concern and exchange with its people, at first as its subjects and eventually as citizens and members of civil society. In turn, the operation of modern civil society has been marked by a progressively active engagement with the state. Normative studies of the relations between government and society have a long tradition, especially strong in the second postwar period. More recently, studying the so-called quality of democracy, in order to strengthen it, has become a cottage industry, recruiting a large number of scholars. Quality democracies are unquestionably democracies formally and *de facto* guaranteeing freedom, the rule of law, political participation, political equality, competition, vertical and horizontal accountability, and responsiveness (Diamond and Morlino 2004).[1] Unquestionably, all of these qualities have to do with two aspects of the government-society pairing. They have to do with the proper set-up of each, and with the proper set-up of their relations. Without a doubt, in sum, proper government, proper society and proper relations have been at the core of what makes a democracy authentic. So much for norms and aspirations. Who would not agree? But there is a complication. Each of these norms and aspirations is broadly stated and therefore lends itself to different interpretations. Further, there is an unprecedented difference in the way in which norms were interpreted until the close of the last century, and the way they are understood today by a number of national and international systems of governance. This essay is interested in the impact of these differences upon present national democracies. Historically, how did matters stand, in norms and aspirations, and in practice? And how do they stand today?

I begin with the present day; I will then go back to the past. Speaking of proper government, proper society, and proper relations as understood today and practiced in the West, I wish to recall the often quoted statements which two major democratic leaders issued toward the closing of the last century. In 1981, in his

---

1. The place of these dimensions within democratic theory is, however, not as simple as their plain interchangeable listing may suggest. Some of the dimensions are part of the very definition of democracies; others are conditions. There are also issues about their relative importance, their relations, their interpretation, their practical application. Further, different dimensions address different normative issues. But I am not interested in dissecting these normative questions. I am interested in the significance of recent transformations in democratic government, in civil society and in their relations.

first inaugural address, President Ronald Reagan declared, 'In this present crisis, government is not the solution to our problem; government is the problem'. On September 23rd, 1987, the British magazine *Woman's Own*, in an interview with Margaret Thatcher, British prime minister since 1979, reported the following statement by the prime minister, '[People] are casting their problem on society. And you know what, there is no such thing as society. There are individual men and women, and there are families [...] and people must look to themselves first'. Thatcher repeated the statement almost verbatim in her speech at her party's annual conference of the same year. Placed side by side, the two statements by Reagan and Thatcher converge in impeaching democratic government, civil society and their close, long-standing interaction as understood and operating since their very inception. They offer a completely different, deconstructing perspective on what had been considered and practiced as proper in all three aspects. Reagan's and Thatcher's were emphatically resonant statements, but uttered by two world political leaders they were more than mere rhetoric. In fact, they announced the final entrance of so-called neoliberalism in the life of advanced democratic states and their citizens. As a set of beliefs – anthropological, social and political as much as economic – neoliberalism goes back to the immediate postwar period. As practiced by international organisations, in programmes of international assistance and in the restructuring of dependent and peripheral states, neoliberalism became operative sometime before the 1980s. But it is only in the last thirty years or so that neoliberalism has come to display the full range of its ambitions and achievements: its pervasively 'creative destruction' of the politics and collective life of advanced democracies.

Certainly, the paths to neoliberalism have not been uniform, sequential and ordained; its geographical development has been uneven; different traces and combinations of it are found in different countries, in domestic and global organisations. An unmitigated cogent display of its achievements and ambitions is found among Western democracies, and more so in the United States than in the UK. Hence, this essay will devote progressive attention to the United States as an exemplary case of what is at stake. The essay does not study the history and global causes of neoliberalism. Rather, it wishes to observe its operation, its capacity for destructive creation, and the construction of its appeal. As to the external causes of neoliberalism, I limit myself to the observation that neoliberalism, not just as a doctrine but more importantly as an active political movement and a system of governance, developed from a concerted reaction to the objective crisis of advanced global and financial capitalism of the 1970s.[2] With the help of David Harvey (2005), who offers a synthetic but well-documented analysis of the earlier developments in the global politics of neoliberalism, I buttress the observation with a 'history in time' remark. The stagflation of the 1970s came at the end of a half-century stretch during which, in the United States, the income of common

---

2. The reader who wishes to go beyond this quick analysis may find an excellent guide to the structural causes the 1970s' crisis in Mark Blyth (2002).

people grew, while the share controlled by the highest earners fell and remained restrained after the war and the economic expansions that followed it. Harvey comments,

> While growth was strong, this restraint seemed not to matter. To have a stable share of an increasing pie is one thing. But when growth collapsed in the 1970s [...] then upper classes everywhere felt threatened [...] [I]n the 1970s [the control of wealth by the top 1 per cent] plunged precipitously [...] The upper classes had to move decisively. [...] (Harvey 2005: 15)

And move they did; reversing, with the decisive assistance of developing neoliberal policies, their decline. Blyth (2002) offers in this regard a comparative analysis of the 1930s' and 1970s' great transformations and the contrasting interests (labour *vs* business) they respectively mobilised and served.

But the unfolding of neoliberalism following the 1970s came, more significantly, from the construction of powerful alternative ideas pushing to replace the Fordist consensus with a new narrative. It is to this narrative aspect, and to its intellectual pedigree, that I will devote special attention throughout, because narratives can act, and did act in the case of neoliberalism, as performative agencies; they can fulfil their task by the compulsion of their declaratory display. Pierre Bourdieu announces the neoliberal feat as follows,

> What if [neoliberalism] were, in reality, only the implementation of a utopia [...], thus converted into a political programme, but a utopia which, with the aid of the economic theory to which it subscribes, manages to see itself as the scientific description of reality. (Bourdieu 1998: 94)

Utopia in epistemological garb turns itself axiomatically into ontology, and programme.

I stated that neoliberalism's notable achievements and its still unrequited agenda are intentionally and formidably destructive. They are also ambitiously creative; but creative of what, exactly? Neoliberalism, so-called by its intellectual founders for its alleged roots in neoclassical economics, is not only an economic doctrine for the purposes of running an economy, it is at the same time, and above all, a way of governing a country and a way for upright citizens (Thatcher's statement) to conduct themselves. As an economic doctrine, it borrows from monetarism, public choice and supply-side. In theory and in practice, economic neoliberalism pursues a free-market fundamentalism. But its pursuit, when convincingly attended to, has a range that goes well beyond the free exchange of material goods and services. It embraces a vast spectrum of political and societal conducts; it embraces their operations and their operators. It involves enclosing much of human action (I choose the verb on purpose) within the logic of market choices; it involves redefining within that logic what makes human operations and operators proper and natural. In human affairs, market-like competitive choices are proper, responsible and ultimately liberating. Is this not what modernity is all about? And is neoliberalism not a return to the roots of modernity? Or is it?

To show how revolutionary neoliberalism has been in reshuffling and indeed deconstructing the relations between state and civil society, I will revisit the ways in which we, political scientists, have variously theorised and tested those relations since the postwar growth of our discipline. In the process, I will offer my own reading of those theorisations and how neoliberal norms and practices overtook them. World War II marked the defeat of Fascism but also the expansion of Communist rule behind the Iron Curtain. In answer to the painful memories and the lingering realities of assorted Twentieth Century dictatorships, postwar students of democracy turned their main attention to the empirical-theoretical assessment of the conditions favouring the development and consolidation of democracy. They stressed the overlapping pluralism of society and the autonomy and diversity of its various social and economic components as the two necessary conditions for democracy. Whether what was necessary was also sufficient received comparatively less attention. Testing the conditions of democracy relied especially on behavioural, cultural-attitudinal, interest group and structural-functionalist approaches. These approaches soon came to dominate the field of political science in general. The approaches and their claims differed in many ways; yet, from their different perspectives, they all converged on the preeminent democratic importance of richly articulated civil societies. Civil society was conceived not as a congeries of separate individuals and their kin (Thatcher) but as an interactive set of primary and secondary formations freely attending to their own pursuits; hence, also capable of placing themselves as a relevant public sphere *vis-à-vis* government. From this perspective, the state and its institutions appeared as a sort of transmission belt or an other-directed black box. It was sufficient to study what society transferred to the box in order to know what would come out of it. Presumably, to study what went on within the box did not add much knowledge to democratic theory.[3] Or, at best, attention to government institutions was limited to their function, in a sequential division of labour, as aggregators of the demands that the public sphere articulated. Aggregation was itself mainly conceived and documented as the task of political parties, themselves construed as a bridge between politics and society. It is no coincidence that, among the rules of the democratic game, electoral laws became a flourishing field of studies in political science.

Thus, with one interval which I discuss later, special attention to civil society has been a constant of empirical democratic theory since World War II. However, while in the first years after the war, scholars tended to focus on documenting how the autonomy of civil society was contributing to the success of postwar democratic governments, following the fall of right-wing dictatorships in the 1970s, and more so the fall of Communism in 1989, civil society attracted attention for its role as a censor and antagonist of distant unresponsive and arrogant governments. The change of emphasis is in part explained by the peaceful role that civil societies

---

3.   Therefore it did not add to the prestige and research resources of those who ventured to study the black box; not as much as would be added by following the paradigms prevailing at the time.

decisively played in the fall of the remaining European dictatorships; a peaceful role they did not play in the military defeat of Italian Fascism and German Nazism. Successful antagonism toward oppressive governments helped lifting civil society from a necessary condition, a component, of democratic government to the Lockean embodiment, spontaneous, innovative and honest, of democracy itself. The new perspective found a receptive echo in the West, where distrust of governing institutions and professional politicians, often spurred on by the cultural upheavals that began in the late 1960s, was already spreading (and even today shows no indication of abating). To anticipate, suspicion of democratic governments fits comfortably, as we will see, with neoliberalism's populist evangelisations.

Did the shifting of attention from a politically trusting to a suspicious civil society make a difference for democratic analysts? And if it did, what did the difference consist in? For some analysts, an autonomous civil society, while necessary for democracy, is compatible with trust as well as with Lockean distancing from government. For others, as in Robert Putnam's analysis of declining social capital in the United States (1995), a decline in the richness of an interactive civil society ('bowling alone') went together, without fully explaining it, with falling trust. For yet others – and I place myself in this category – the emphasis on civil society as a necessary and sufficient democratic condition appeared overplayed and reductivist. After all, contrary to many analyses of the collapse of the Weimar Republic, German civil society was lively, articulate and unquestionably outspoken. Theories stressing civil society were, in effect, incomplete. They were incomplete or inattentive when, as in postwar functional theories, they placed greater stress, for analytical but also civic-political reasons, on the stabilising functional role of overlapping social pluralism than on the dysfunctions of internal social conflicts. Dysfunctions became, by deduction, nothing more than the destabilising flipside of functional equilibrium. Theories were incomplete when – as for instance in the cases of William Kornhauser (1959) and Hannah Arendt (1958: 315–23) – they explained why social conflict ushered democratic collapse by arguing deductively: Weimar was a mass society, and in a mass society social conflict is dysfunctional. They were incomplete when treating government as a transmission belt and overlooking its possible role in triggering popular discontent.

On the last point, in the 1980s there was finally a revival of attention to government and state institutions (the coined phrase called for 'bringing the state back in'), spurred on by, and in turn spurring, a decline of the behavioural paradigm (Evans *et al.* 1985). After all, the study of institutions, administrations and public legal systems went way back to the origins of political science as a discipline. The revival offered an opportunity to look anew to the state as a relatively independent resourceful agent, called to insure, together with civil society, the legitimate operation of democracy. The revival, however, suffered from a problem of timing. Renewed attention to the state came on the heels of the increasing distrust of government and professional politicians, felt not only by the public but also in intellectual and political circles. The object of distrust was not generic. Fed most forcefully and successfully by emerging neoliberalism, distrust specifically impeached the model of twentieth century mass democracy, in the operation of which civil society and government institutions had progressively converged during a long stretch of that century. Hence, impeachment placed the practitioners and advocates of a more government-centred model on the defensive. The critics of the model had now set the ground and terms of discourse.

What was the model concretely about? What did civil society and government converge on and share? What they shared is best revealed not so much by recourse to postwar empirical democratic theories as by recourse to much earlier turn-of-the-century macro-sociological theories of modernity, modernisation and the modern state. They had offered a scenario of government and civil society under modernity that still allows us to make, in my view, better sense of the way fully developed democracies eventually came to operate. Modernity speaks the language of formal rationality, and formal rationality is what government and civil society came to share. Placed within rationality, the autonomy of civil society is a resource against subordination. However, other than that, autonomy does not declare its uses. It allows us to confront government, but confrontation with public institutions is not the rule. Elections, political parties, interest groups, labour unions and cooperatives, media, civil political and social rights, are not in themselves tools and arenas designed for antagonism. In sum, to stress the unquestionable autonomy of those who are governed from those who govern them, and vice versa, may not be the best way to capture the actual relations the two entertained during a large part of the past century. In Max Weber's disenchanted analysis, the modern state and its bureaucratic apparatus was only one of the sites within which the iron logic of modernity asserted itself. It was the most striking, resistant, wilful embodiment of formal rationality as the final architecture of modernity. But beyond the state and partially without its assistance, modernity also moulded, conditioned and, in fact, ordered the individual as well as the collective, the private as well as the public, society as well as the state. Modernity and rationality reveal the common context within which state and society, each within their role and with their own resources, each with its own sense of institutional appropriateness (March and Olsen 1995, especially pp. 154–56), came to interact, communicate and, especially in the postwar era, sustain each other. Jürgen Habermas (1991) captured the place of civil society in the operation of this pairing in his concept of *Öffentlichkeit* (Public Sphere). The public sphere, as a historical premise for the political formation of liberal and liberal-democratic government, would prove itself the 'institutional hinge between state and society' (Gianfranco Poggi, personal communication).

I spoke metaphorically of formal rationality as the architecture of modernity, embracing state and society. Michel Foucault, closing his 1978–9 lectures at the Collège de France, takes that architecture back to the times of Machiavelli, when

one no longer tries to peg government to the truth; one tries to peg government to rationality [...] It [becomes eventually][...] a matter of modelling government on the rationality of those who are governed [...] as subjects of interest in the more general sense [...] [T]he rationality of the governed must serve as the regulating principle for the rationality of government. (Foucault 2008: 311–12)

It could be said that, in so writing, Foucault goes beyond Weber. To say the least, government and society seem to be placed together as prime movers in defining the criterion for proper behaviour under modernity. In the course of this essay, I will return extensively to Foucault. In a nutshell and to anticipate, Foucault's accent on the pervasiveness of modern rationality is central to what he calls the art of government, or also *gouvernementalité*; it is central to the disciplined conducts, in Foucault's terminology, of *homo oeconomicus* and his government. Together with Weber, the French scholar offers us a convincing narrative of how state and society converged in the conduct of government. That convergence is now challenged by the practices and the narrative of neoliberalism and neoliberal governments. Weber and Foucault assist us in unravelling the nature of the challenge. The challenged convergence was predicated on the reciprocity of conducts and embodied in what I shall call the government of the social with (that is, jointly with) the social. It implies a shared Foucauldian discipline. Because the discipline is collective and reciprocal, neoliberalism takes it to be a source of dependency. Neoliberalism proposes to subvert it by replacing it with another discipline - presumably a liberating one because under it the individual initiates and is solely responsible for his own behaviour and choices; he carries, alone, the burden of their consequences. It follows that, in neoliberal preaching, government is an odious necessity to abstain from as much as possible (but neoliberal governance, as we shall see, cannot and does not practice abstinence, quite the contrary). It also follows that society as formulator and carrier of collectively relevant commitment is like government considered a hindrance to individually free agency.

State-sponsored social welfare is the first obvious target of neoliberal attack, as it is both financially unsustainable and individually degrading. 'Welfare' and 'social entitlements' become negatively loaded terms. The social dependency they foster is to be replaced by the rise of an 'ownership society'. But ownership of what and by whom? George W. Bush, in his speech to the 2004 Republican nominating convention, announced, 'Ownership brings security, and dignity and independence'. The statement would seem uncontroversial, if it weren't for the fact that the president was not referring to the private ownership of real and personal goods but to the privatisation, that is the personal assumption, in sum the 'ownership', of social risks (pensions, health, disabilities, unemployment [...]). The individualisation of social risks is not just a presumably necessary economic measure; it is above all an ethical principle – personal as much as civic. As a prophet of a natural, spontaneous ownership society, neoliberalism also welcomes low taxation as a principle, since money earned by the taxpayer obviously belongs to the taxpayer, who will best know how to employ it in his own and hence everybody's best interests.[4] At the same time, government must and can learn to live sparingly,

---

4.   As to the money we pay in taxes, it certainly is our own money, but to paraphrase Marx's famous dictum on history, 'men make their own [money], but they do not make it just as they please; they do not make it under circumstances chosen by themselves, but under circumstances directly

the more so as some of its functions (those worth preserving) are better performed if no longer guided by the bloated logic of bureaucratic rent but by the lean logic of the market. Hence the increasing use of private outsourcing and contracting out of even the most defining functions of the state in matters of defence, justice, law and order. Hence the introduction of New Public Management's market-oriented efficiency as the superior criterion guiding the public sector.

To conclude, just as postwar theorists of democracy finally turned their attention to the unique role the state had played in the proper operation of twentieth century democracies, neoliberal ideology impeached that state and neoliberal policies attended to deprive it of its prerogatives. And when neoliberal action is accompanied by the often repeated and rehashed statement that government is not the solution but the problem, it is not surprising that public distrust of government achieves epidemic proportions. But if the government is up for private sale, who exactly are those who bid for it, and why do they bid? What does the new management promise; what does it achieve? As to civil society, what can it do when left to its own liberating devices? Does it take over? Alone? With what resources: political, economic, legal? How does it redefine its internal relations? And by what criteria? What happens to the old criteria? Margaret Thatcher's statement that society does not exist raised hackles, not only on the left. So she tried to explain it away. She insisted that society as a whole was an empty abstraction to which we nevertheless appeal to justify demands for protection. But she added that society was instead '[…] a living structure of individuals, families, neighbours and voluntary associations […] [I]t was a source of obligation' (Thatcher 1993: 626). Put this way, the statement is sufficiently innocuous. However, that living structure is neither a welcome fact of nature nor the spontaneous product of individual initiatives. In the modern legal-rational state, that living social structure cannot actually exist, prosper and act without the assistance and indeed the cascading incentives provided by legal rules and public policies that capacitate and channel it. The same is true of instruments like markets and competition, the operation of which is in no way natural, spontaneous and ideally without guidance. I just

---

encountered […]'. Among the circumstances assisting our moneymaking, there are some that justify why we pay taxes and explain their use. *See* the analyses offered by Lian Murphy and Thomas Nagel (2002) and by Stephen Holmes and Cass Sunstein (1999). Their analyses are based on legal positivism: in the legal-rational framework of the modern state, private property is not explained nor does it survive by reason of natural rights. It is explained and is sustained by legal convention. It is the product of positive law, which defines, regulates, protects and fosters it. It follows that what we produce and gain as private individuals is produced with the costly assistance of the state. Murphy and Nagel write, 'To appeal to the consequences of a convention […] as a fact of nature which provides the justification for that convention […] is always to argue in a circle' (Murphy and Nagel 2002: 9). The illustrations offered by the authors are never-ending. I add that what we produce as private individuals, and what we consequently possess, relies on a vast range of infrastructures and services that, collective by definition, only public institutions appropriately financed are in the position to offer to one and all. For instance, justice is a service which only qualified state institutions can and must offer. But if we cut the part of the justice budget that is devoted to free legal assistance, if we cut the services offered by public defenders, an indigent defendant may end up being condemned because he is without a defender.

described public incentives for a prosperous civil society as cascading. I mean by this that the effects of public policies, even when policies appear to be of secondary importance for civil society, can go well beyond the matter on which they rule. They are often meant to spill over on the organisation of society as a whole, on the way in which society places itself in the political arena (Soss *et al.* 2007). One of the best examples is offered by fiscally pursued redistributive policies. Redistribution of wealth is not their ultimate goal but a means to other goals, a way, for instance, of influencing or discouraging individual or group conducts. Hence my rhetorical questions: is it not reasonable to expect that the distal effects of neoliberal public policies in regard for instance to the personal assumption of social risks may, consciously or unconsciously, discourage Thatcher's spontaneous living structures? Is it not possible that, by placing ostensible trust in those structures' capacity to flourish when left to their own devices, neoliberal policies will end up producing the opposite? Is it not possible that those policies will eventually fragment, discourage and humiliate those living structures; some of them intentionally more than others? If government is not the solution but the problem, what do we get in exchange?

In the last two sentences, I have once again placed state and civil society side-by-side: the neoliberal impeachment of the state beside the disempowering of a society left to its own devices. What holds the two together under neoliberalism is the flattening of both state and civil society on market-driven criteria; the removal of the public sphere as the discursive arena where society meets government. Incidentally, it seems to me that the type of meager civil society that neoliberalism envisions, in which the best citizen is the one who competitively takes care of himself, would not have done much for the overthrow of Communism. Fortunately, even under dictatorship, the civil society that neoliberalism, and many others, hailed for its role in the collapse of Communism had apparently much more going for itself.

Chapter Two

Social Risk in Early Modernity: Solidarity as Precaution

From Weber to Foucault: 'governing the social with the social'

Like the proverbial bumblebee, modernity, surprisingly, flies, sort of. To be sure, the bumblebee is the same as ever; modernity is modernities, it changes. Still, even as it changes, modernity appears to remain a strange construction, complex and demanding, difficult to operate, almost unnatural. For Mark Lilla, modernity has the downright fragility of children's fiction,

> [...] modernisation, secularisation, the 'disenchantment of the world,' 'history as the story of liberty,' [...] These are the fairy tales of our time. [...] They serve the same function [...] that tales of witches and wizards do in our children's imaginations: they make the world legible, they assure us of its irrevocability, and they relieve us of responsibility for maintaining it. (Lilla 2007: 6)

But is a fairy tale only a fairy tale? If it is only a fairy tale, why, how and in what form is modernity still with us? It forced us to be free: from traditions, from religions, from myths, from ascriptions. In so doing it did give us in exchange the opportunity to reach for a secular dignity *an und für sich*, but it also marked us, in Weber's phrase, with the 'disenchantment of the world'. It mobilised us, it put us to work, it compelled us to reflect on whom we wished to associate with, how, and for what. Still, as the story goes, since modernity was not concerned with our own destinies, it left us of necessity without substantive guidance. It offered instead the efficient guidance of formal or instrumental rationality. Under it, modernity presented society as an open arena where we presumably meet in reasoned pursuit of our own earthly agendas. The story implied that, given modernity's individualising logic, oblivious as such to collectively persuasive coagulants, the study of society could be usefully conducted only from the bottom up. It could only focus on means (and ends) that, posited as pertaining to the individual and to alliances individually initiated, would prove mutable, contingent, potentially fragmenting and aimless. If this were the whole story and we were to pause here, then it would fit nicely with neoliberalism's ambitious self-narrative: neoliberalism as a revolution in the original sense of the word, as a return to a betrayed mythical past, as the recovery of modernity's original soul. Indeed, it would fit with neoliberalism's ambition as the self-appointed prophet of what Antoine Garapon pungently calls radicalised modernity (Garapon 2012).

But was modernity betrayed? My story is different. There was no betrayal. The above description of modernity is incomplete. In fact, if confined to the description above, modernity could never have come to be. Modernity endured as modernity because formal or instrumental rationality was not and is not unmoored individual freedom and nothing else. While fostering modern individualism, formal rationality was part and parcel of a larger system of stabilising constrictions, self-imposed and institutional at the same time. The system was born, in Max Weber's analysis, as a secular immanentisation of the Protestant ethic. In order to subject individual actions to virtuous exchange calculations, immanentisation demanded the objectification of others and with it the equal disciplining and instrumentalisation of the self. Further, the rise of the nation state in coincidence with modernity and the Reformation[1] channels and institutionalizes these persuasions, most conspicuously in its bureaucracy. Other factors, no less important for being less conspicuous, also contribute. True, the distinction between modern society and the modern state emphasizes the openness and plurality of the former, the role of the latter in governing society and itself.[2] The state exercises this role by means of formal rationality, best embodied in its bureaucracy and its practices (hierarchy, predictability, certainty, data...). But, equally true, these instruments consolidate a set of behaviours and adjustments that go beyond the state as they also involve, in possibly endured compliance with the state, those groups and individuals with whom the state interacts. Otherwise said, though eventually engaged and framed by the state, there exist individual behaviours and adjustments, the roots of which are not in the state. They are, rather, facets of a generalised psychology and culture of rationality that manifests itself in more diffuse, more or less conscious and purposeful ways: in society, in its aggregations, in the individual. They are facets on their own of secular immanentisation.

Thus, what most closely explains the successful impact of formal rationality is in essence the fact that its practices are constant and diffuse, from the bottom at least as much as from the top. Rationality will eventually permeate the politics of the democratic state; it will situate the choices of each political actor within mass politics, within political parties, within parliaments. But as we continue looking from the bottom up, rationality already permeated, since the dawning of modernity, daily behaviours and practices pertaining to family, work, community, clergy and congregations. It defined the appropriateness of our actions in response to others and defined, with it, our identities. Decisive in this regard is Foucault's opus. Beginning with his 1978–79 lectures at the Collège de France (2008), Foucault focuses his attention on the capillary diffusion of rationality, its instrumental uses and its specificity within modernity. He casts his net wide by reconstructing from the ground up practices of individual discipline,

---

1.   I will not discuss interaction between causes. I prefer to assert that the modern state, pegged to rationality rather than the truth (Foucault 2008: 311–13), is an essential component of modernisation, and that individualism as well as discipline, both pegged to rationality, are only conceivable within such a state.

2.   This does not mean that the modern state was born for the purpose of governing an otherwise ungovernable commonwealth; it means that it ended up doing so. The distinction, though important, is irrelevant for our purpose.

techniques in his terminology, in close (if uncodified) answer to daily personal events and issues. Their rationality is part and parcel of everyday life. There are occasions when this reconstruction of decentralised rationality leads Foucault to explicitly discount the state's role in social discipline, and to discount with it Weber's analysis of that role: self-discipline is so rooted in everyday practices and discourses, that the state, so to say, finds everything ready to hand. In my view, however, Foucault's attention to the capillary diffuseness of practices opens up and enriches rationality, it gives it new, fertile soil, but it does not necessarily subtract from Weber's discourse.[3]

Therefore, I suggest here a different reading, one that accommodates both Weber and Foucault. It is worth noticing, to start with, that Foucault's systematic emphasis on horizontal practices and decentralised discourses actually echoes Weber's earlier emphasis on the individualised immanentisation of the Protestant ethic as a prime motor of modern rationality.[4] Indeed, to gloss Weber on immanentisation, if the Puritan sought signs of salvation in a scrupulous work ethic, we, whether Puritan or not, are now forced to be scrupulous by the ideally prevailing practices of our professions. As to Foucault, his focus on decentralised daily conducts is not incompatible with a more robust Weberian reading of the role the state's disciplinary techniques come finally to play in lending collective persuasion to decentralised practices. The state is advantaged by practices arriving from other contexts; but it also orders and strengthens those practices. It thus gives life to a potentially virtuous exchange between government and society. The centrality of this exchange may be hidden from the scholars by the analytical separations which, as scholars, we espouse between the private and the public, between the formal and the informal, between command and subjection. Foucault himself, in his classical essay on *gouvernementalité* (Foucault 1991b), shows how, starting with enlightened absolutism, the modern state progressively takes on a prominent role in the management and discipline of the social. In the essay, Foucault revisits, with added eloquence, the path from *polizeistaat* to enlightened absolutism. *Polizeistaaten* are at first creatures of cold means, unseductive ends and often uncertain futures. Only some will survive as fully-fledged nation states to be reckoned with, and their survival will be accompanied by a new, purposeful attention to their territory and population.

---

3. Students and followers of Foucault may accuse me of twisting, here and in what will follow, his thought. I plead guilty to cherry picking. But this is the beauty of Foucault: his reflections are so studded with insights, generous but not always cumulative over the years of his career, that a gleaner can suit himself without doing damage to the generous sower.

4. *See* most recently Philip Gorski (Gorski 2003, esp. Ch.1). In his analysis of the protestant roots of the disciplinary modern state, Gorski devotes special attention to the contributions of both Weber and Foucault: Weber, for his emphasis on the Reformation; Foucault, for his emphasis on the horizontal diffuseness of discipline and its techniques. As cited by Gorski, the closing paragraph of Weber's *The Protestant Ethic* stresses 'the significance of ascetic rationalism for the content of socio-political ethics, that is, for the organisational forms and functions of social institutions from the conventicle to the state' (Gorski 2003: 26).

From the absolute to the liberal state: continuities

Foucault opens his essay on governmentality with a transformative distinction between the personalised sovereign reason of the prince, as best embodied in Machiavelli's writings, and the institutional reason to which the absolute state will peg what Foucault calls the art of government. In Foucault, the power which Machiavelli's prince retains is, as it were, unproblematic. It is personal and indivisible; its use can be and indeed must be, when necessary and virtuously employed, forceful and ruthless. This is how power is normally practiced, whether to defend the territory or to mete out justice. The latter is the prince's material justice, bloody when required, applied *in corpore vili* to display and reassert the prince's numinous power. Similarly, in matters of territory the prince looks at his domains from a transcendent relation of sovereign remoteness, seeing them as a fixed resource for the pursuit of his personal agenda. Ordinarily, public-mindedness, tending to the territory and its people, are secondary or extraneous to the prince's reason; they are matters of no consequence. Ordinarily, the prince entertains no desires, capacities or needs to take cognisance of the ways in which collectivities give themselves tasks, sustain themselves on the territory, guide themselves. Ordinarily, the prince is oblivious to other forms and sites of power, dispersed over the territory. He is not impelled to engage and absorb them. He does not need to, as long as the prince's reason is limited to the retention of his domain. Retention, however, may be replaced by ambitions of conquest, or may be challenged by other princes. Mobilisation of resources may be in order. In which case, greater attention to the needs of the territory and its inhabitants may prove to benefit the provident prince. This is where the art of government begins. Foucault captures the transition when he writes:

> whereas the doctrine of the prince and the juridical theory of sovereignty are constantly attempting to draw the line between the power of the prince and any other form of power, because its task is to explain and justify this essential discontinuity between them, in the art of government the task is to establish a continuity, in both an upward and downward direction. (Foucault 1991b: 91)

The pursuit of this two-way continuity did not mean (at least not yet) that society was now in the position to enter into a partnership with the state. Partnership (reciprocal exchange) will take the first steps only as the absolute state begins to decline. Certainly, the dawn of the modern state is the dawn of a way of governing assisted by attention to the economies (their tasks and organisation) of the collectivities that the state now intends to embrace. Still, especially in its early incarnations, the absolutist state, driven first by royal patrimonialism and then more forcefully by mercantilism, differs from its successors by its cooptation and management of those economies. In a *Polizeistaat*, i.e. a police state, it is the state that mainly takes responsibility for the care of the *polis*, for its collective integrity.

State care takes two forms. The first in approximate time is also the more restrictive. Caring for the collectivity means, as for instance in Norbert Elias' analysis of the birth of civility in the modern state (1969; 1982), to ensure that collective conduct obeys rules of civil coexistence in an environment, especially urban, that is temperate, salubrious, orderly, industrious (Dean 1999a: 89–91). It means removing from the community those who, by violating its codes of conduct, endanger its wholesomeness. I spoke of restrictive care because, being concerned with the poor, the marginal, the mentally sick, in sum, those marked as undesirable outcasts, all bundled together for police (i.e. policy) purposes, the state advocates their confinement in appropriately designed institutions (hospitals, hospices, asylums, houses of correction, workhouses). Being restrictive, these police measures actually break with the past. With the immanentisation of the protestant work ethic and the advent of the secularising modern state, the poor, the beggar, the disabled and the itinerant cease to be, even in Catholic countries, the medieval image of the suffering Christ eliciting Christian charity. They are now a social problem. They are a source of economic fragility, because they are unproductive, but above all, of moral disorder at a time when poverty is not seen as the result of external circumstances but rather of sheer idleness, slothfulness and vagrancy. In point of fact, the work that the above total institutions imposed on their inmates, most often the slothful, was not necessarily productive, yet it was always intended as a reminder of individual failings and, at best, as a means of possible individual rehabilitation. I do not know whether Italian sayings such as 'sloth is the father of all vices', or 'work ennobles' man date back to those times: they stress, at any rate, the ethical value of work.

While inscribed in the first, the second form which care of the *polis* takes goes beyond it. The *polis* of the modern state is progressively the site of an unprecedented economic revolution, at the discursive centre of which stands eventually the productive importance as well as the ethical value of regular employment. It progressively makes sense to speak of idleness not just as an individual moral problem but more and more as a collective problem of work and productivity, of employment and the supply of the employable. Therefore, the second form of state care is the fostering of community welfare, for economic as much as for moral reasons. Now, the fostering of community welfare aims less at shielding a defined and fixed productive community (by removing, and thus potentially making more idle, the idlers and vagabonds), and more at actively enriching the community and its capacities by managing the pool of capable workers.[5] Actionable knowledge

---

5. The sequence I just presented simplifies a more complex reality. Here, for instance, is a signifi-cant if relatively short-lived exception to the linear sequence just described. In England, earlier sixteenth century attitudes toward poverty – attitudes common to other Reformation countries – had been punitive and often confining. However, at the turn of that century, the English parlia-ment approved two acts requiring parishes to provide largely 'outdoor' relief, that is, without compulsory confinement in detention structures, to the sick, the old, the orphans, the unemployed whether or not able-bodied (wage subsidies for poor agricultural labourers followed at the end of the eighteenth century). Then, following the decline of British mercantilism and the 1832 Reform Act, granting the franchise to the middle classes, the 1834 Poor Law Reform Act overturned outdoor relief and wage subsidies, because of its allegedly perverse effects, and replaced it with extremely punitive compulsory detention (poorhouses) and hard work (workhouses) policies (Mencher: 1967 Chapter Six). The reform law was variously intended to shame and remove,

about the community at large is essential in these regards. Knowledge starts with the systematic search and collection of data concerning society's sources of dangers and opportunities, of risks to avoid or to invest in. Thus, the fostering of communal welfare no longer relies on the *Kadi*'s traditional justice dispensed substantially case by case, as Weber describes it. Rather, it aims at collective policies, the formulation of which is assisted by statistics. Born to serve the *polizeistaat*, hence its name, statistics is the collection of data embracing both society and the state.

Thus, the beginning of the modern state witnessed a hybridisation of the law. The law was conceived originally as the will of the sovereign, which the jurists normalised by turning it, in the double meaning of the term, into norm. It now embodied expertise, rationality, assisted by technical knowledge (economic, demographic, engineering, military, medical, criminal). Law becomes legislation and regulation, at times preventive. I am suggesting that contemporary awareness of realities no longer in the grip of tradition, and reliance on a public calculus of utilities, are all conducts with a long history behind them. The conducts manifested themselves with modernity and remained long uncontested. Their central task was and is to measure and broach the unavoidable risks and opportunities of modernity, within modernity's codes. Already under the enlightened versions of absolutism, patrimonial conceptions of royal government became objects of internal conflict between monarchs, military and civilian bureaucracies, and judicial bodies. In Prussia between the eighteenth and nineteenth centuries those conflicts were among the factors that led, during the Napoleonic occupation, to top-down agrarian, military and administrative reforms. They did not constitutionalise autocracy, they certainly did not project society to the centre of politics, but they slowly signalled a retrenching of patrimonial rule, the professionalisation of civil bureaucracies, the lawful removal or the withering of ascriptive criteria for access to land markets and professions.

---

but also to induce its subjects to amend their ways by making the new forms of relief so brutal as to turn them into a deterrent. As one of the commissioners of the new poor law wrote, 'No relief shall be given to the able-bodied, or to their families, except in return for work, and that work shall be as hard as it can be made, or in the workhouse, and that workhouse as disagreeable as it can be made'. Compared to the subtler reeducation policies adopted, as we shall see, by contemporary neoliberalism, these are explicitly nasty means indeed. It is interesting to read the New Poor Law the way Karl Polanyi (1957 [1944]) read it, as a first neoliberal, or in Polanyi's language, socially disembedded experiment. As a brief experiment, it preceded instead of following, as in its present American version, the conquests of socially conscious movements. In England, labour and socially conscious conservatism followed the early nineteenth century neoliberal experiment; in the United States the New Deal and the New Society preceded today's neoliberalism. English justifications of the Reform Act, arguing on one side the perversely pauperising Malthusian effects of the Elizabethan acts, appealing on the other side to social naturalism and the inherent superiority of market spontaneity, took the form of a new narrative, similar to the narrative of contemporary neoliberalism. Margaret Somers and Fred Block (2005) offer an impressive and tightly constructed comparative analysis of the two neoliberal or, in the authors' language, market fundamentalist experiments. While the authors point to the similar politico-economic antecedents of the two, they focus their analysis on the finally decisive role of ideational factors, articulated by authoritative thinkers and think tanks, in propelling neoliberalism/market fundamentalism.

If not under absolutism, then under the liberal and more fully under the demo-bureaucratic state, society and the state will converge in the deliberative process. The give and take of proposals and expectations, of demands and responses, resolves itself in a language, the language of public policy, that government and society share. The language is shaped and gains substance by the growth of the state apparatus but also by the diffusion, with feedbacks, of codes of conduct in the schools, hospitals, barracks, prisons and other total institutions. Thus, the law, as Foucault puts it, is governmentalised.[6]

It is here, in his embracing notion of governmentality, that Foucault adds to Weber. Under modernity, power is for Weber the exclusive prerogative of the state. It is legitimate; it is public authority. The modern state absorbs, centralises, and monopolizes powers once retained by many. Power becomes political, separate and dominant with respect to other sources and forms of power, and the relation between the state and its subjects (no term is more appropriate) remains one of unproblematic command. The issue of its legitimacy is, for Weber, an issue of legal rationality, civilised but buttressed by force. Foucault offers a more complex, more embracing and richer, but still unforgiving, narrative. The richer narrative has two sources. The first source is a double constant. For Foucault, power is always associated with knowledge, and knowledge with power. In Foucault's famous statement: 'There is no power relation without the correlative constitution of a field of knowledge, nor any knowledge that does not presuppose and constitute at the same time power relations' (Foucault 1977: 27). This recursive system gathers strength from the horizontal diffuseness, the plural clustering and the routinised persuasiveness, as it were, of disciplinary techniques. However, while their diffuseness and persuasiveness are also a constant, the techniques may themselves change, because different knowledge, different discourses about power, may come to underlie them. It is here that the second source of Foucault's more embracing narrative resides. For him, the secularisation of knowledge that accompanies modernity also potentially disperses and decentralizes knowledge and learnt disciplines. If power and knowledge exclusively in the hands of the prince had been unproblematic, the transition to the modern state begins to problematise power, its sources, sites, tools and justifications, by problematising the knowledge and the power that the state is called to display.

---

6. This first part of my essay reflects the European more than the American experience. Worth notic-ing is the fact that in American politics and American political science we speak of government, whereas in Europe we speak of state. In my American teaching I often asked students what they meant by 'government'. With some goading on my part, the answers were a veritable grab-bag: the president, Congress, elections, federal state and local administrations, political parties, judges at all levels, labour unions, professional associations, interest groups, lobbies, popular initiatives. There are ample historical and constitutional reasons why the vast denotation of the word govern-ment makes instinctive sense in the United States. Be that as it may, to think of European states as governments, in the loose, all-embracing sense above, is a practical way of understanding the importance of all the components of government. I remember, as a student of jurisprudence in Italy, that interest groups were never taught because they 'did not exist'. That is, they had no legal status in the eyes of the State on high.

Parenthetically, according to some critics, Foucault, by conceiving of power as everywhere present because it is rooted in many different producers of knowledge, normalises power in the very act of conceptualising it (Fraser 1981: 272–87). If power is knowledge and knowledge is power, everything then is licit, or for that matter illicit, or a-licit. There is no issue of legitimacy. If everything is discipline, how are we to distinguish between dominion, force and violence on the one hand, and sovereignty, authority, legality and legitimacy on the other? Also, how can we distinguish between public and private, between spheres of state competence and spheres that, with liberalism, the state itself will actually be called to protect from public interference? Foucault's emphasis on discipline – even when discipline is dispassionate, civilised and normalised – would seem to cast an unsettling shadow on the modern art of government. Mitchell Dean writes, 'The notion of sovereignty directs our attention to questions of legitimacy and consent; that of discipline raises one of normalisation though corporeal training' (Dean 1999a:170). Being only an opportunistic gleaner in the field of Foucauldian studies, I do not propose to delve into the many issues that these critiques raise with regard to Foucault's notion of governmentality. I am satisfied to recall that Foucault's stress on the power-knowledge pairing is also a stress on the plural, beyond the state, sources of knowledge. The persuasiveness of state action does not rest on some ascribed portentous quality of state knowledge. It rests, as state action is deployed, on continuous secular tests of its import. In turn, actions thus tested give credit to the state. This is in fact the thesis advanced and verified by Seymour M. Lipset (Lipset 1960: 77–83). The popular legitimacy of the democratic state gains from its verified performance, and performance, in turn, is eased as legitimacy builds up. Under modernity, knowledge exclusively declared from the centre of the state, that is, knowledge exclusively appropriated, eventually turns into debased and debasing knowledge; it turns into an accounting system that pretends to be non-controversial.[7] Rather, a modern state gains credit to the extent that its actions embody knowledge and speak a language that its communities of reference share and to which they contribute. This implies, again, that under modernity the collection and elaboration of knowledge, and its employment as a guide to conduct, are at their best when society and state converge; when they meet in the art of government.

Until recently in the history of the modern state, we have as a matter of fact witnessed a considerable intensification of that convergence. I pointed out that the first signs of convergence are found in the enlightened phase of absolutism and in the early stages of liberal states. But during these phases, the mobilisation of state bureaucracies and society was of small import in comparison to the weight of the commonwealth, government and public sphere combined, under mass democracy. Initially, liberal thought and practices embraced civil society

---

7.   In this sense, modern dictatorships are modern more in timing than in essence. Their centralised knowledge is not knowledge pursued; it is an accounting system with eventually disproved pretenses of infallibility. Turning politics into administration was in fact Communism's intended goal.

as their only sensible arena. They conceived of it as mainly a free, disinterested and occasionally (Masons) exclusive venue, in which to document and contest, in speech and in writing more than in action, the pervasive paternalism and self-referentiality of traditional dynastic rule. Beyond this educational mission, liberal thought showed wariness at the prospect of taking over and exercising power. Wariness is explained in part as a reaction to the practices of state power that liberals, like everyone else, were subjected to. European liberals, continental more than British (but think of Burke), also shared early on, to further their wariness, a broader conviction that any state action, no matter in what form, no matter by what kind of state, was unnatural because it would interfere with the stability of society's presumably spontaneous, self-given social order.[8] It would evoke the spectre of an uncalled for and threatening Leviathan. All of this helps explain why many liberal regimes tarried, once in power, in addressing gathering social issues. However, it stands to reason that, had liberal regimes in power remained hesitant about its exercise, had they remained anchored to a defence of the public sphere and of civil society as disdainfully removed from the state, they would not have been able to govern, except by somehow abolishing the state. They would have been unable to offer a necessary alternative to states past, since the alternative required imagining liberalism as government fostering a liberal public sphere going beyond a discursive, contesting function.

Eventually, the skeptical minimalism of liberal regimes receded. The change of mind, the rethinking of the liberal mission in government and society, came about in response to the slow coming apart of the traditional structures and strictures of society. I suggest that minimalism receded, for one thing, thanks to those accumulations of newfangled knowledge by, in, and about society that the governance of the *polizeistaat* had, willingly or unwillingly, already *de facto* facilitated. These accumulations disproved assumptions or expectations about the nature of society; those which the *polizeistaat* entertained (society as a *tabula rasa*, a passive subject of rule), as well as those entertained by early liberalism (society as the pristine natural counter to the state). Thus, under liberal governments, civil society gains voice, power and identity, takes roots and normalises itself not so much by the vigor of pre-existing ideations which early liberalism did not contemplate. Rather, society gained voice thanks to the multiple paths through which it mobilised knowledge: in part autonomously and from the ground up, in part in response to, or by the impulse of, government. Society began to derive and accumulate knowledge and propositive ideas, conducts and power, from the experience of regulated markets, from statistics and demography, from producing and consuming, from epidemiology (a field in rapid expansion in the second part of the nineteenth century), from the growing prevention of risks: medical, working, urban, environmental. These webs of knowledge wove new alliances, attuned to and tested by the reading that prospective partners shared of that knowledge. Therefore, to say that liberal governments governed 'less' than

---

8.   I will return to the presumed naturalism of society when dealing with neoliberalism.

all-knowing royal absolutism does not mean that they paid less attention toward all things social. At issue, when we say 'less', is the mode of governance; one that, under liberalism, is more discursive, propositive, experiential. And it means, to return to the terminology heading this chapter, that government is progressively government of the social together with the social.

Chapter Three

The Century of the Social State

Moving now to the turn of the twentieth century, we find that the government of public affairs devotes more and more attention to the social challenges stemming from the dramatic growth and transformation of capitalism. Responses and public policies found resonance in reform liberalism, reform socialism (social democracy), the labour movement, red and white syndicalism, Catholic and sociological (Durkheim) solidarism, as well as socially alert conservatism and, in the United States, in philosophical Pragmatism and the Progressive Era. In T. H. Marshall's analysis (1964), this is the period during which social rights gain ground, in response to the impersonality and insecurity, physical, economic and contractual, of labour and industrial relations under capitalism. There is something unique in social rights, when compared to civil and political rights. The latter are individual, universal and, once legally achieved, non-controversial in principle, because they are the constitutional guarantees without which a competitive system does not exist and cannot operate. They were conquered after a long and hard-fought journey, but once conquered[1] they affirmed themselves by definition. They protect the exercise of autonomous individual choices in the public as much as in the private sphere. At the same time, unless competitive systems are themselves on the verge of being overthrown, civil and political rights will not constitute the main issues of contention. Compared to them, social rights do not define a method. Rather, they define and expand a field of central and legitimate contestation among progressively and rightfully equal contestants. I describe contestants as progressively equal because the first traces of public attention to the social are already situated in the *polizeistaat*'s concern with the conduct of commoners and then with their welfare; well before welfare mutates from a bureaucratic concession into a fought-over popular conquest and a negotiable entitlement.[2] Social rights may apply to everybody (universal health coverage, where universality favours, incidentally, its legitimacy), but more often than not they apply to specific classes and conditions. The enjoyment of some of them may be recurrently subject to means testing as well as to budgetary and other policy considerations. That is, they are material commitments, economic, fiscal and financial, calling upon the state to assume their budgetary costs or to allocate them among the intended social beneficiaries. In order to be collective,

---

1. In Germany they will actually be conquered well after Bismarck's 1880's social legislation.

2. Despite the negative connotation recently attached to the word as meaning something undeservedly appropriated, the pristine meaning of 'entitlement' is rightful title. A welfare entitlement is the legal claim to a good or service designed to protect the holder from external risks.

enjoyment of entitlements must go together with equally collective commitments, in budget lines, transfers, taxes and fees, and also in co-payments and insurance contributions. 'Social rights', Maurizio Ferrera writes in this regard, 'must be sustained by unrelenting sharing acts. This is why they rest on a specialised organisational form: that of compulsory social insurance' (Ferrera 2005: 46). The evident advantage of legal sharing in social security systems is to make the often unforeseen and unsustainable costs otherwise falling on less fortunate citizens into costs sustained in solidarity by the larger community. Solidarity, as in the title of this chapter, is broadly precautionary; it protects the larger society, inclusive of those who at the moment are not exposed to risk, by protecting those who are. Solidarity policies do not require that governments take over; they do not require that, as single providers, they assume full control or carry the full burden. Even without these strict requirements, the policies are still in the position to address social disparities and risks tied to specific demographic, health and occupational conditions. In so doing, solidarity policies also forge new identities and new impulses to political mobilisation and political alliances. To put it in the scholarly narrative employed by early studies of the welfare state, at a time when welfare was still a word with positive connotations, social rights did not remove the inequalities of capitalism, they curbed them, they remedied their negative effects, and as a consequence they contributed to capitalist consolidation. Class conflict was tamed by what the French notoriously called *concertation sociale*. Unsurprisingly, in the eyes of turn-of-the-century revolutionary socialism and subsequently in those of Marxism-Leninism, the same development revealed social democracy's betrayal of the class struggle.[3]

From its beginnings, government of the social with the social presented two features of import. First, it offered ways to stabilise and normalise the domain of social contention; one that, for a good part of the twentieth century, advanced democracies were called to address and manage. The domain embraced the substantive policies, the composition and roles of the contestants, and the processes to be followed in the definition and pursuit of those policies. Second, the meeting of government and social constituencies was accompanied by and further affected

---

3. Indeed, in the 1930s the Comintern denounced social democracy as social fascism. Perversely, there was something to the claim. In a review article, Robert Paxton (2013) reminds us that 'All the modern twentieth-century European dictatorships of the right, both fascist and authoritarian, were welfare states'. And he aptly comments that '[t]he current conservative American agenda of a weak state associated with *laissez-faire* economic and social arrangements would have been anathema to them, as an extreme perversion of a despised individualistic liberalism (in that term's original sense)'. I already pointed out that Bismarck, following the outlawing of the Social Democratic Party, was first in Europe to introduce social legislation. All of this does not escape some neoliberal politicians and commentators critical of president Obama's Health Care Plan, who denounce it as an obvious first step toward the government's takeover of everything. Lunatic fringes have raised the spectrum of Obamacare as a slippery slope toward Eugenics, death panels, a new Holocaust. A perfunctory search of the Web will quickly reveal a wealth of such lunacies. Lunacies? Friedrich Hayek, in the opening pages of the *Road to Serfdom* (1944), made a similar point about the British Beveridge plan as a slippery road toward British Nazification. Such is, according to him, the dynamic of all states.

the reorganisation of those constituencies, the way in which they came together. An early example of these reorganisations is the appearance of mutual aid societies, mutual savings banks, people's cooperatives with various functions, all of them often connected to political parties, labour unions and other mass organisations. They competed with and challenged private charities and philanthropies, religious reliefs and fraternities of old. Did it make a difference? Private and religious charity organisations usually individualised risk; they often treated the victims of risk as carriers of risk. They addressed them as passive subordinates, called to atone and make amends.[4] Instead, secular solidarity gave risk and solidarity a collective dimension, it offered reasons for inclusion and mobilisation, it provided stimuli to political action. Solidarity and its constituencies became central to the politics of twentieth century mass political parties and their collateral organisations, including secularised Catholic parties, and hence to the politics of governments that political parties may take to task but also run or aspire to run. The reshuffling of societal relations brought about by the government of the social disproves once more the belief that society has a stable natural order of its own, tampering with which is useless, dangerous or counterproductive. On the contrary, it proves that society is a work in progress to which many different people attend. During most of the twentieth century, these transformations occurred not only in European democracies, including Lib-Lab England, but also, in its own ways, in the United States.[5] In the USA, where mass politics had already begun to take shape during Andrew Jackson's presidency (1829–37), there were two periods in particular during which issues of social solidarity gained a voice. They were the period of Progressivism, at the turn of the twentieth century and, beginning in the thirties, the New Deal.[6]

---

4. Some of them inherited the New Poor Law's moralising zeal. Some (temperance leagues, often run by women), presented their programme as one of social reform: rescuing workers, their families, their women, their children, and their families from the bane of drinking. Drinking, as the saying went, is the curse of the working class. Or, to put it in Oscar Wilde's upside-down world, *work is the curse of the drinking classes*; where, by drinking classes, Wilde most probably intended the loafing, bibulous golden youth of *fin de siècle* London clubs – a sort of total, though voluntary, institution. Wilde's witticism was attributed by others to a witless Oxford Don, best known for his droll mangling of the English language.

5. Constitutional systems play an important role in the way in which social issues are articulated by governing institutions, political parties, other organisations and associations. In the United States, federalism and local government in general discourage the vertical, hierarchical structuring of political parties, representative institutions and interest groups. They also resist the federalisation of public policies. A macroscopic example is the legal and regulatory difference, interstate and state-federal, in the American treatment of crime.

6. The literature on the latter is endless. A recent contribution is found in the introductory chapter of the volume edited by Soss, Hacker and Mettler (2007). Its value for this essay is in its compendium of the ways in which, beginning in the seventies, neoliberal policies came to subvert the New Deal's policies of solidarity.

Shared understanding and narratives

I will explain in the central part of this section how, following the developments described in the previous section, both the civic practice of holding government accountable and the governments' practice of giving account of their actions came to be normalised. Certainly, normalisation is no guarantee that the conduct of the two practices proves itself impeccable. Suffice to read what Diamond and Morlino, in their essay on the quality of democracy (2004), write on the matter. The two authors decry a long series of what they see as clearly unauthentic conducts, fairly common to all democracies, including established ones. The recurring conducts include dissimulations, ambiguities, half-truths, spinning, sound bites, unsubstantiated claims, manipulations of information; all of this on the part of public officials called to scrutiny by voters and stakeholders who are themselves divided by conflicting demands, perspectives and expectations. There is no denying the existence of such conducts. Indeed, the picture of shortcomings the two authors draw reminds me of the scepticism that critics of Athenian democracy expressed at the time toward its practice of *parrhesia*, i.e. toward speaking straight and without fear, speaking the truth *coram populo*. According to the one criticism among many that the critics offered, in Athens *parrhesia* did not pay. It was more expedient to tell others what they liked to hear, even at the cost, as the critics saw it, of lying. But was it lying? If the audience does not already embrace the speaker's truth, the speaker may at times find it helpful to dissimulate, to be ambiguous, to appeal to sound bites and similar rhetorical artifices, of the type that Diamond and Morlino berate. However, in an open democracy, not all dissimulations, ambiguities and half-truths are shortcomings and nothing but shortcomings. Judith Shklar writes,

> The paradox of liberal democracy is that […] the politics of persuasion require […] a certain amount of dissimulation […] On the other hand, the structure of open political competition exaggerates the importance and prevalence of hypocrisy because it is the vice of which all parties can, and do, accuse each other. It is not at all clear that zealous candor would serve liberal politics particularly well. (Cited in Morozov 2013: 122)

For her part, Deborah Stone comments,

> Ambiguity enables the transformation of individual intentions and actions into collective results and purposes. Without it, cooperation and compromise would be far more difficult if not impossible […] Ambiguity facilitates negotiation and compromise because it allows opponents to claim victory from a single resolution. (Cited in Morozov 2013:123)

These are frequently everyday devices of persuasion which democratic actors routinely employ in times of routine democracy.

But, twisted as it may sound, the routine acceptance of such devices of persuasion still demands that we share a common language. In order to give audience to a public person, whether or not we will like what he or she says, it is necessary to share a language that gives collective sense to realities that we all experience. Reciprocal understanding, a shared language, defines the nature of the issues we want to talk about.[7] Language, to say the least, mediates reality. As an instrument of presentation and persuasion it therefore "persuades" reality. Further, the language we share, because it needs to be shared, is subject to impermanence. This is the key in which I read Foucault's words in the last of seven recorded seminar lectures on the meaning and evolution of *parrhesia* in Greek and Roman civilisations (Berkeley, October/November 1983). The theme of the lectures was *Discourse and Truth: the Problematisation of Parrhesia*. Foucault closed the lectures with the following comment:

> What I tried to do from the beginning was to analyse the process of *problematisation* – which means: how and why certain things (behaviour, phenomena, processes) became a problem. Why, for example, certain forms of behaviour were characterised and classified as 'madness' while other similar forms were completely neglected at a given historical moment; the same thing for crime and delinquency, the same question of problematisation for sexuality [...] There is the relation of thought and reality in the process of problematisation [...] [I]t is this kind of specific relation [...] which I tried to analyse in the various problematisations of parrhesia.

The task that Foucault proposed requires that we ask ourselves why and how some phenomena, manifestations, conducts that lacked a nexus at certain times or in certain contexts, acquired it subsequently: why they came to be joined, defined, treated, and possibly regulated under it. The question is how they acquired a meaning of their own; how they managed to represent truths on which we eventually engaged – how, in sum, they were problematised. Where phenomena, manifestations, and conducts acquire a nexus in our minds, there the subjective nexus asserts new knowledge and with it, the potential for new power. Applied to what surrounds us, knowledge provides new problem-solving tools. We can speak of problematisation as an epistemic turn, with an emphasis on problem-solving constructivism. Problematisation is also *re*problematisation. An old nexus, old ways in which we gave sense to fragments of reality by joining them, are replaced by new ways and newly constructed knowledge. Somers and Block label 'epistemic privilege' this capacity of constructing knowledge anew (Somers and Block 2005: 265).

Examples of reproblematisation are unending. The private use of one's public office for personal gains – today a crime – was, in the West, part and parcel of recognised prebendary systems. Decrying it as an inherently reprehensible source of interest conflict would not have made much sense; as a class and a term, interest conflict did not apply. Equally, conditions and statuses such as disabled, handicapped, homeless and transgender were, in the past, differently named, and accompanied by (often fully accepted) forms of repression, discrimination,

---

7.   Suffice to think, in this regard, of the importance American Pragmatism assigned to problem solving and, to begin with, to the collective definition of what constitutes a problem.

criminalisation and even death. In the past, the word *castigamatti* was used in Italy as a proverbial substitute for cudgel, to refer to its recommended punitive use on insane-asylum inmates. Those same marginalised human conditions are today a source of social concern and of protective and human rights policies. Strikes and other forms of labour action, in the past repressed, legally as much as illegally, progressively became and remained (until recently) the foundation of social rights. A good example of reproblematisation, finally received in the laws, is the overturning during the New Deal of American constitutional jurisprudence on work protection. Until then, the Supreme Court had been the last bulwark of continuous resistance to the labour policies already sponsored during the Progressive Movement.

The dominant discourse that comes to characterise the democratic government of the social in the twentieth century represents the final act of a slow process of reproblematisation. There is, as I repeatedly stressed in previous sections, a line of inherited continuity in the normalisation of social-democratic discourse on the treatment of the population. The history of social rights, the resonance of inequalities as begetters of social insecurity (and vice versa), the accompanying reorganisations of civil society, and the progressive expansion of the welfare state are all matters known, studied and revisited at great length. What I wish to emphasize is the fact that the evolving processes aimed at the control of social risks converged on, and therefore normalised, conducts and disciplines that came to be shared by citizens and governments. I return here to the theme of persuasion, as part and parcel of a shared language. Attention to the presence (or absence) of such language should enrich the study of sources and conditions of 'accountability' and 'responsiveness'. When we assess the two – in a way they are the same obligation seen from the respective perspectives of government and society – we habitually do it by seeking guidance in the separate analytical components of genuine liberal democracy. We emphasise formal guarantees and the precious autonomy of each of the parts, public and private. We rightly stress not only the autonomy between the parts but also the internal autonomy of their own components; the controls to which public institutions submit each other as well as the pluralism of social groups and personal autonomy. All of these are the building blocs of democratic living, of its own legitimacy. They are also and in particular the paths by which the government of the social by the social seeks authenticity; thanks to a constant critical scrutiny of the codes by which each one of us – institution, group, and individual – operates and interacts. But, in the final analysis, that authenticity resonates only if and when we share an understanding of the issues on which we contend, that is, when the issues are framed by a common problematisation.

I should like to recall in this regard the teaching of Seymour Martin Lipset. Writing more than half a century ago about democratic legitimacy and performance, Lipset remarked upon and offered quantitative evidence about the fact that the two are empirically correlated; they help or, when one is absent, undermine each other. In his interpretation of the data, Lipset pointed out that poor performance may eventually erode the legitimacy that an established democracy enjoys (Lipset 1960: 77–83). What to do to avoid the predicament? It is not a mere coincidence that Lipset formulated his answer at a time when government of the social by the social held sway. Lipset answered by recalling the extension of political and then economic and social citizenship (the right to collective bargaining in particular) as starting points in the consolidation of Western democracies. He wrote, in the language typical of the political sociology of the fifties and sixties,

> [...] where the workers were denied both economic and political rights, their struggle for redistribution of income and status was superimposed on a revolutionary ideology. Where the economic and status struggle developed outside of this context, the ideology with which it was linked tended to be that of gradual reform. (Lipset 1960, p. 85)

That is to say that democracies gain legitimation if and when both social contestants and governments, fairly irrespective of which party governs, believe that the policies regarding social and economic rights are central to the performance of a democracy. Democracies gain legitimation if the shared belief helps identify, in a context of common problematisation, accepted criteria by which performance will be assessed.[8] This was, at the time, the essence of gradual reformism or social-democratisation. Assisting these developments were the aggregative capacities that, at the time when Lipset was writing, mass political parties possessed. Those capacities made control of the administration of public affairs more feasible, actions of governments more ponderable, speaking one's mind more amenable to reward. Therefore, performance as a source of legitimacy was the more powerful because the largest social constituencies converged in the assessment of social policies, including the opportunities they offered for the reorganisation and empowerment of society.

I have retraced, in the last few pages, the research path that Lipset, and subsequently many more, thanks to him, pursued. In retracing Lipset, I have added, with the help of sociologists of modernity like Weber and Foucault, a critical dimension that, in Lipset and in the dominant political sociology of the postwar era, had no special reason to be. It concerns the rationalisation of collective action and the disciplining of our own conduct, both of which are a mark of modernity. Discipline and rationalisation, together with the articulation of democracy as government of the social with the social, offered the normalising context for a way of staying together under modernity, between individual freedom and collective needs, which, to recall Mark Lilla, is otherwise precarious. It was certainly not the context for carefree forgiving behaviour of the type now promised by a misplaced conception of civil society as naturally free, critical, and unrestrained by the discipline of the state. Let me add that the conception is, fortunately, not only wide of the mark. Also, there is nothing rosy or particularly creative about a society as simply a bulwark against external subjection. Taken to its extremes, to embrace

---

8.   Years ago, I defined performance as follows: 'The term performance refers to [...] the manner and effectiveness with which something fulfills an intended task [...] Performance, to put it redundantly, is effective to the extent that it produces what is intended' (Di Palma 1977: 7).

such a view is to subvert any discourse of collective conduct, whether fostered by the state, or indeed by society and by our own communities. It is, in sum, to subvert society. This closing reflection serves to alert us to the potential impermanence of that way of living together under democracy, combining individual freedom and collective needs, which has accompanied us until the dawn of the new century.

Etsi coactus, tamen volui [9]

In order to prepare for next chapter's treatment of that impermanence, I take the lead from what Gianfranco Poggi writes on the legitimation of the political power exercised by the democratic state. Poggi condenses his understanding of that legitimation by borrowing the Roman civil law brocard *etsi coactus, tamen volui*. If the brocard captures in its terseness the reason underlying legitimation, in what sense is it right and truthful? Poggi focuses on two aspects of the maxim. The first one regards why we accept to obey. The second and more interesting regards the fact that, according to Poggi, we are not in the position to accept (or obtain) obedience until and unless we understand each other, we share a common language; specifically, the language of individual and collective responsibility; the language that tells us what responsibility is all about (Poggi 1990).

The well-known answer to the first query, why we accept to obey, resides, says Poggi, in the modern state's rule of law, which lends authority to its command. We accept an external command because the modern state legally commits itself to the impersonality, neutrality and predictability of its laws' policies and actions. Through the law, the modern state, as Norbert Elias put it, civilizes itself. Let me add that the democratic state's increasing attention, during the twentieth century, to solidarity and redistribution contributed to removing 'systemic errors' historically favouring the better-off. The removal of systemic errors added substance to the formal impartiality, neutrality and impersonality of the rule of law. Lipset would have explained that the removal of systemic errors contributed to democratic legitimation. In fairness, the pairing of performance with legitimation does not go without criticisms. Adam Przeworski (1986: 47–67) tersely captures the essence of the criticisms. For him, performance is everything, it is measurable, and it is all we need to know in order to understand voters' responses. Legitimacy and related concepts, such as loyalty, allegiance, trust and consensus, are pleonastic, as they postulate the existence of a subjective disposition that is indemonstrable, probably nonexistent and unnecessary to boot. Legitimacy stands in for a demonstrable interest calculus and nothing more. His analysis is razor-sharp but not uncontroversial. More modestly, I am satisfied with recalling that I opened this section speaking about power, command and obedience, about their normalisation under the rule of law. But I moved my emphasis to shared performance or (better) to societal partaking in performance, its pursuit and its effects, and thus to the societal contribution

---

9.   *Though compelled I willingly accept.*

to its persuasiveness. Persuasiveness may be a way around Przeworski's epistemological problems with legitimacy.

Compared to persuasiveness, words such as dominion, coercion, monopoly of violence, punishment, or expressions such as 'do as I tell you, otherwise...', used in reference to the exercise of political power, are less innocent. They are loaded and not to be used lightly. For one thing, they suggest a zero-sum view of political power, according to which it is rational, rewarding, efficient and safer to accumulate power by taking it away from others or preventing others from obtaining it. But this view is questionable. Were we to accept it, a number of institutional arrangements of power would make little sense: checks and balances, federalism, the increasing weight of the judiciary, the exclusive power of central banks. According to some recent analyses, especially by American constitutionalists and legal scholars, the existence and evolution of these and similar features is part and parcel of a perspective on political power, applicable even to some authoritarian judicial systems (Ginsburg and Moustafa 2008), that emphasizes instead the systemic rewards of parcelling out responsibilities by parcelling out power.[10] It could be countered that at least some of these institutional restraints, in particular those that characterise American democracy as a compound republic, were adopted precisely to remedy a natural zero-sum use of political power ('if men were angels'). But were the founding fathers correct in their zero-sum view of power?

Those loaded terms (dominion, coercion, violence) conjure up a distorting and downright reductive image of the instruments and practices of supposedly civilised governments as actually punitive or at least unduly constrictive. They suggest an opposition between power and freedom, either one or the other, that assigns the two to reciprocally exclusive domains. I wrote above that democratic power and its games cannot logically exist without freedom. The two domains are

---

10. The weaker systems, the systems that show themselves unable to manage the complexity of governing with society, are dictatorships, not democracies. Despotism only survives if it manages to cling, uneasily and unimaginatively, to undivided power, oblivious of individual feelings. There is a page in Alessandro Manzoni's *I promessi sposi,* in which Cardinal Federigo, Milano's archbishop, reproaches at length Don Abbondio, the novel's cowardly country curate, for having succumbed to the iniquitous demands of the novel's petty tyrant. One of Federigo's reproaches is that: 'iniquity may, indeed, have threats to employ, blows to bestow, but not commands to give' (Manzoni, [1825], 1909: 439). Like the Christian martyrs, who refused to convert, Don Abbondio was indeed free to disregard the threats. Similarly, the inquisitor, by displaying the torture's paraphernalia, offers the heretic a choice. He can 'confess' and prevent his suffering, or he can refuse, and suffer the consequences. A refusal is the more disappointing for the inquisitor, as a confession given, true or false, is a confession true by definition (it is an *auto da fé*). A somewhat different case is that of the secret services torturing the presumptive spy or terrorist. Here, since the secret services aim, habitually, at obtaining the real truth, a confession extracted under duress might have nothing to do with the truth, and could actually put the secret service on the wrong track. In such a case, the torturer would obtain the same result as the dictator: manifest obedience but intimate refusal. With this in addition: with the inquisitor, and indeed the dictator (Kuran 1995), a public lie is convenient and sufficient (*oderint dum metuant*). This is not necessarily so for the secret service.

different, without being exclusive. Foucault is quite eloquent on the matter and deserves to be quoted at length. According to him, power,

> [...] does not exclude the use of violence any more than it does the obtaining of consent [...] But [...] in itself the exercise of power is not violence; nor is it a consent which, implicitly, is renewable [...] Power is exercised only over free subjects and only insofar as they are free [...] Consequently there is not face to face confrontation of power and freedom which is mutually exclusive (freedom disappears everywhere power is exercised), but a much more complicated interplay [...] Freedom must exist [...] since without the possibility of recalcitrance, power would be equivalent to a physical determination. (Foucault 1982: 220–21)

As to the second aspect of Poggi's adopted brocard, his decoding of *tamen volui* is on the same wavelength as Foucault on power and freedom,

> [...] a command is a thoroughly intersubjective operation: by means of it one subject seeks to initiate and control another subject's activity. It also [...] presupposes the other subject's ability to entertain and interpret the message addressed to him/her [...] On account of both [...] every command implicitly acknowledges that compliance with it is, when all is said and done, a contingent matter, requiring both that it be properly understood and that the person to whom it is addressed be willing to obey it. (Poggi 1990: 6)

The statement, similarly to Foucault's treatment of power and freedom, helps us understand how the language of political power can be routinised in the language of everyday public policies, their laws and regulations. That *tamen volui* is no more an expression of obedience borne under threatened duress than the words that precede it (*etsi coactus*) expresses a *dour aut aut*. In the language of everyday public policies, the brocard captures instead the unadorned facts of shared compliance with the norm, where norm (as in the Italian expression *mettersi a norma*) has the double meaning of legal rule and measured average.

I close this chapter by restating my lengthy story about the democratic government of the social by the social. This type of government came to characterise the twentieth century and reached its apex during the first decades after WWII. It situated itself between discipline and freedom, between rule and choice, between consent and debate. With it, the exercise of political power was made possible and credible by the freedoms of the citizens who were exposed to that power. Their freedoms were, in turn, protected by that power. For a good stretch of the last century, we witnessed freedoms next to discipline, personal conducts marked by both individual autonomy and collective responsibility. All of this has been given significance by the enduring presence in civil society and the state of a common discourse; a discourse problematising the social risks that complex modern societies carry with themselves as risks that, morally and materially, can best be addressed in solidarity. Echoing Durkheim, Garland explains why solidarity requires a partnership of state and civil society:

Social arrangements [...] [of modernity] pose acute problems of social order and call for the creation of governmental institutions and civic associations that can build social solidarity and ensure moral regulation. Complex societies need more organisation, not less, and while markets can organise economic efficiencies, they do little to bring about moral restraint, social integration, or a sense of group belonging. (Garland 2001: 101)

And so it has been. It is therefore not surprising that, when that necessary partnership is challenged in the most radical way, when that partnership is denounced as imposed by the state and detrimental to a free society, when a radically alternative problematisation of social risks is successfully advanced by neoliberalism, the consequences are subversive.

What now?

Chapter Four

Social Risk in an Era of Uncertainty: The Dismantling of Solidarity

As Yogi Berra, baseball legend and *gaffeur*, put it, 'it's tough to make predictions, especially about the *future*'. Nonsense? A quip? If I remove the adverb, the assertion states, rather redundantly, a fact, plain and simple. If I add another quip by Yogi, 'things ain't what they used to be',[1] the fact is one that deserves attention. The future may indeed prove itself to be in some fundamental way different from the past and present. From this, it follows that uncertainty, even ignorance as to what to expect, may ensue and cause concern. We may feel at risk. How do we protect ourselves, what precautionary measures are there? Under normal circumstances, the expectations that common mortals as well as equally mortal elites entertain about the future are projections, almost instinctive, of past and present experiences as they have assimilated them; in other words, we go by, and in a way rely on, the same old recipe, the same old dish.

In view of the fact that nowadays few of us, whether experts or common mortals, seem to put much faith in the old recipe, either because it is no longer at hand or because we do not put much trust in it, I deduce, with possibly hasty logic, that nowadays *mala tempora currunt*.[2] I described in the first chapter of the essay some of the troubles recently wracking state and society. These troubles have instilled in all, scholars and citizens, the sensation of being witnesses to radical transformations. Yet we are uncertain about their long-run import, their direction, their social and moral implications. I could proceed by simply discussing the present troubles, the uncertainties that accompany them and the various interpretations offered in the relevant literature. It would be a prudent way of proceeding, since it cannot and should not be the task of the social scientist, or anybody else, to advance generalisations about the extended future. However, it is one thing to try and predict a future state of affairs moving from realities now in turmoil, it is another and more approachable thing to try and give some order to those realities, to conceptualise them as much as possible. The latter way of proceeding would be less akin to political science proper than to what Giovanni Sartori calls political theory (Sartori 1987: 15–18). It does not do away with 'political science', but it logically precedes it by framing what is at issue. One additional clarification is in order. I will frame the realities in turmoil as subjective ones. Insofar as the turmoil introduced in the first chapter finds expression in practices, conducts and

---

1.   It is also the title of a piece by Duke Ellington.

2.   *Bad times are upon us* (Google translation).

policies, in sum, in actors' reactions, they exhibit strong subjective components. These components are the most reliable and revealing as to the consequences, but the consequences do not fulfil historical necessities. QED.

By subjectivities, I mean the way we experience ongoing transformations, the way we live with and by them, the way we deal with them. Transformations, facts and realities in general, are not unquestionable events; they do not speak for themselves. As events, they enter the scene with a plot (a *canovaccio*) more than a script. But the unfolding of the plot has much to do with the audience's feedback – and the audience is diverse, in composition and in reactions. The current transformations both in state and in civil society discussed in the first chapter engage two subjectivities. One is in civil society. It consists, as is well known, in the diffuse sensation that the government of the social with the social (the conduct of conduct, in Foucault's words), the public commitment to policies of collective protection from social risks, is challenged and is otherwise becoming obsolete. It consists in the reactions induced by that sensation. The second subjectivity is the one that, as I just suggested, triggers the first. In the closing words of the previous chapter I referred to it as neoliberalism's subversive reproblematisation of social risks in contemporary societies. Packaging itself as an ideology claiming a distant pedigree, neoliberalism successfully conducts reproblematisation by way of a novel method of governing.

I begin with the first subjectivity.

The veil of the future, from premodern to modern

If normally we see our future as a projection of the way we have lived so far, and if 'so far' actually means a long stretch of time, then the projection is automatic and un-reflexive. But if that long stretch of time seems to come to an end, if, unaccountably, things seem to us out of the ordinary, then the sense of uncertainty as to what we expect next, the lack of direction, and the inability to project from the past they all become the more troubling. The normality that is nowadays in doubt was centered, as I have said, on the policies of solidarity as protective measures from the social risks and the collective as much as individual costs induced by industrialism. That long-lasting problematisation no longer works. I just announced but have not yet developed my thesis: the long-lasting problematisation has been giving way to the reproblematisation advanced by neoliberalism. But before developing the argument, I wish to understand how people who are used to collective protection from social risks react personally when that protection is challenged. I will do so by starting with reflections on the historical relations between perceptions of the future and perceptions of risk and risk protection.

As ordinary people in ordinary times, the perception that we tend to have about the quality of our lives, especially its safety, and the lives of people like us, is closely connected with how we see the future, how far we project it, and with how much and how intensely we think about it. As ordinary people, we may live the future as a daily projection of today, and that projection may be no better than a resigned compendium of everyday worries. In this case, the future promises at best nothing new and invites us to look no further. Alternatively, the future may be the object of medium-range feasible calculations with which we manage to live. Thirdly, we may construct the future in a longer perspective, as distant, hazy, and uncertain beyond what we accept, and therefore as a source of new worries, possibly repressed.[3] It stands to reason that before modernity the future, either immediate or medium-range, was not a topic that invited priority reflection and calculation. The future was impenetrable, and for most a useless or scary subject upon which to reflect. The reasons are infinite: daily cares, hunger and diseases, pandemics and epidemics, lack of information, lack of resources, physical isolation, fears, constantly dangerous surroundings, fatalism and tradition. If at all, remedies were sought in witchcraft, in superstitions or in religion's promises of life after life.[4] There was a comforting quality about some of these remedies. By implying that history was preordained, they exempted most people and 'organic intellectuals' from the trouble of understanding history as the uncertain product of human actions, and therefore from the need to deal with uncertainty, with reason and foresight but also with risks and aggravations. As to the promises of religion, the Church of Rome's promise of eternal life took good care of the future, by evasion, a fugue in the otherworldly – the sinner shall be damned, the innocent will be rewarded – that did away with any reflection on the future as inherently uncertain. Like Rome's promise of eternal life, so also utopia, eschatology, millenarian and messianic escapism and similar otherworldly myths, they all lifted us. At times they promised the return to a long-lost idyllic past (communism, anarchism, pastoralism). And if pressed by time, the seer, the oracle, the sibyl, the witches, or an obliging or tormented ghost could exceptionally tear asunder the veil of the future for a selected few.

Protestant monotheism broke with the promise of salvation by faith and in so doing helped set up subjective conditions for the secularisation of future-oriented human action.[5] Modernisation, rationalisation and its practices, as well as the weight that these practices acquired as they converged in the state, aimed

---

3. There is a fourth way of thinking about the future and its risks. It falls, however, outside the continuum, just introduced, between the three ways above. I will treat it at the end of Chapter Seven, in the context of a contemporary increase in the expectations that health risks are avoidable; an increase stimulated by newfangled, unprecedented medical advances. In general, an increase in expectations actually increases risk resentment and unacceptable fears.

4. Before concluding that religion is the opium of the masses, Marx aptly explained that religion 'is [...] the expression of real suffering and a protest against suffering. Religion is the sigh of the oppressed creature, the heart of a heartless world, and the soul of soulless conditions' (Marx 1970 [1843]: 127). In a way, Marx keeps being quoted out of context.

5. The bulk of early science fiction – from the modernist utopia of Bacon's *New Atlantis* to Jules Verne – was probably the most untamed expression of the secular optimism that accompanies the modern scientific revolution. But in the first postwar period (Fritz Lang's *Metropolis*) science fiction also projects the fears for the calamities that may accompany progress. And already in the early nineteenth century (*Frankenstein*) romanticism prefigures the horrors that human defiance of the laws of nature may bring about.

to remove the veil of a preordained yet unknowable future. Historical studies took a new turn as they gained conscience of these transformations and their significance for the discipline. With the transition to modernity and the rise of the state, historical studies, at the time the closest anticipation of the emerging social sciences, worked out a new perspective on the concept of time. With modernity, time 'accelerates', time collapses. During the classical era, the times of history, and the times that history's scribes (Polybius, Thucydides) scanned were long. They were marked by events that tended to repeat themselves uniformly, events that hardly distinguished themselves for novelty and transformative capacities. Alternatively, the same events were compressed into recursive cycles, the only ones that history could conceive. As history accelerated, the idea of change by human action, the idea of a new future at hand, open but reasonably accessible, came to replace millenarian predestination and utopia, the non-place.[6] In the modern state, risk and uncertainty as products of modernity could be subject to calculus, and calculus could in principle frame risk and uncertainty as an issue of collective security. And so it eventually came to be, as state and community came to commit themselves to solidarity policies of risk distribution. These are medium-term expert policies, open to verifications and adjustments and indeed to reasoned debate as to the probability of various risks, their distribution over time and populations, and their costs and the costs and benefits of solidarity action.

This is not to say that calculations as to facts on the ground and expected outcomes are noncontroversial. It means that there exists, or existed until recently, a broad agreement on the kind of variables on which and with which to intervene; an agreement conducive to discussing the social and fiscal impact of the available policies. What is subject to changes over time (from liberal regimes to the welfare state) or among social constituencies is the relevance of some variables, including who participates and who requires assistance. How, for instance, should non-unionised workers or workers with temporary employment be protected. The issues are actually of particular importance today, given contemporary transformations in the nature of production and employment, but have a long history behind them. Other changes over time concerned the values assigned to costs and benefits, and the pondering of probable outcomes. All these changes are understandable. The issues, difficult to measure and evaluate, are budgetary, fiscal and economic, but they are not the only ones. In a system meant to reconcile freedom with collective discipline, responsibility and broader moral concerns, there is also the fundamental issue of how to achieve reconciliation.

It could be said that until recently we lived in a form of democratic organisation which Mary Douglas and Aaron Wildavsky described, in their volume on risk

---

6. The contributions of Reinhard Koselleck (2002) and his school are fundamental in this regard. Koselleck situates the transition to modernity in the straddling period (Otto Brunner's *sattelzeit*) between 1750 and 1850. Koselleck describes this period as characterised by politicisation, democratisation and the invention of ideologies. All three are occasions for new historical timings, for concept formation as the unique product of modernity, and for new languages of science.

and culture, with the inadvertently Foucauldian adjective of 'hierarchical'. By hierarchy, the two authors meant not the rate of vertical authority but an inclusive concentric relationship between individual and community. On hierarchy, they cite Louis Dumont, according to whom 'a hierarchical relation is a relation between larger and smaller or more precisely that which encompasses and that which is encompassed' (Dumont 1970: 105). In the words of Douglas and Wildavsky, 'the characteristic of hierarchy is that all parts are oriented toward the whole' (Douglas and Wildavsky 1982: 90). Years later, Douglas clarified what hierarchy's orientation toward the whole involved: 'Hierarchy does not necessarily perform better, but it is capable of being more aware of minority interests, because it is a political system for incorporating subgroups' (Douglas 1992: 41). To include and incorporate means to avoid the inequalities and unpredictability that ensue when protection from social risk, even if accompanied by publicly supported incentives, is left to individual initiative. It means that coverage is offered as a collective and peremptory good/service, not as a marketable item that profits its supplier. Another statement by the two authors comes handy: 'Contrasted with hierarchy, we use "individualism" for the behaviour that includes market and sustained private profit-seeking of all kinds [...] [A] hierarchy is more tolerant than a society of individuals' (Douglas and Wildavsky 1982: 90–91). Tolerance is paired with precautionary security; security with a future manageable in common.

The risk literature, from modern to postmodern

I announced above that *mala tempora currunt*: that nowadays our views of the future are no longer reassuring. The discomfort is different from the grey resignation about daily life that before modernity induced us to mentally 'remove' the future. It is instead a sense of ongoing uneasiness which we project into a future that is secularly distant and uncertain; but how distant and uncertain we do not quite know. The nature of the uneasiness is mundanely captured in an improvident comment made during the 2008 American presidential campaign by former Republican senator Philip Gramm, at the time economic advisor to the Republican presidential contender John McCain. In a snub to the voters' and the experts' fearful reactions to the 2008 economic recession, Gramm burst out in a 9 July 2008 interview to the *Washington Times*, 'we have sort of become a nation of whiners. You just hear this constant whining, complaining [...]'. He dismissed those reactions as plainly and simply an unreasonable case of 'mental recession'. The hapless former senator had put his big foot in his diminutive political mouth. Still, in speaking of a 'mental recession', Gramm captured, unbeknownst to him, something real and big; he captured the symptoms of something that goes well beyond the effects of the economic recession. It is in fact true that, to put it in the gratuitous language of the former senator, we have become a bunch of whiners, but there have been, there are, and there continue to be plenty of good reasons for it. They are reasons that concern even those among us who, in the immediate future, do not feel (at times because of improvident residual illusions) personally affected by the recession.

The good reasons for worrying about the future stem from ongoing major transformations, veritable historical accelerations in the conduct of advanced democracies. They are above all the well-known transformations in regard to their social purposes and to government-society relations. Indeed, the 2008 economic recession that, starting from the United States, expanded abroad, is in itself only the most tangible and immediately alarming (if only partial) consequence of those political transformations. Modern historians have long ceased to be history's scribes, and social scientists have never subscribed to the task of recording. So it is not surprising that an extensive self-styled critical literature has in recent times essayed to come to terms with these accelerations by interrogating itself on their nature and causes, on their subjective components, on their relations (if any) with transformations in modernity, as well as on the need for new ways of framing and giving sense to the transformations. One of the best known, for academic popularity and interpretative ambitions, if not for empirical support and ease of confutation, is the literature on so-called risk society. A risk society is typically a late-modern society characterised by a constant concern for the increasing risks that supposedly accompany late modernity. I intend to pay attention to the risk literature because some of it reflects not only on the hazards and insecurities generated by social, economic, cultural and environmental features that especially characterise late modernisation, but also on what is, to me, most important, i.e. the public policies and other collective and individual conducts both contributing and reacting to those features. Ulrich Beck writes, 'risk society [...] describes a phase of development of modern society in which the social, political, ecological and individual risks created by the momentum of innovation increasingly elude the control and protective institutions of industrial society' (Beck 1999: 72). Here, risk has a negative connotation: it implies danger, it does not imply opportunity. It is not risk that is worth taking, given the probabilities and the value of the returns, it is risk always to be avoided as its uncertainty regards the probabilities and extent of the damage, as well as the availability of expert remedies to it.

I will employ the risk literature as a thread to guide me through a good portion of the essay. I find it useful for the interpretations it offers, but also for the lessons to draw from its limits. It is useful in the first sense as it invites me to explore the extent to which the concern with risk that marks today's risk society reflects far more than the objective increase in the sources of risk. It also reflects a concern with the fact that the historical treatment of social risk as an issue of solidarity is now being subjected to ideological and policy challenges. An objectively present and diffuse risk is not necessarily a socially relevant risk. Risk becomes relevant when, becoming aware of it, whether or not it personally touches us, we wish to avoid it or intend to confront it with collective measures. These are measures that, in protecting those who are exposed to risk, are meant to lend added safety to the entire community. In principle, a community, or whoever is in charge of it, may well prefer to deny or ignore a diffuse risk, even one that is collective in the positive-choice sense of the adjective (if the risk is present, no individual alone is able to take precautions and avoid it). One good example is government disregard for the serious ecological risks represented by the construction of mega-dams in

China. A risk likely to affect a class of people sharing the same condition may, on the other hand, also be dealt with individually: I will build myself a fallout shelter, even if there is public money available. As to the others, it's their problem.[7] In addition, coping with a risk affecting a class of persons may legally be left to the initiative of each person in that class, even if some cannot afford the cost. In some countries, unemployment is covered by way of collective, compulsive or negotiated, short or long-term, generous or thrifty, unemployment insurance; in other countries it is not.

In the literature, we can distinguish two types of risk. There is the risk to be further examined throughout the essay, i.e. the 'class' risk that follows from industrialism. This risk is still with us, but some of its sources have changed, as has the composition of the affected classes, as well as the way in which we understand class risk. As a consequence, but also (and more revealingly) as a cause, the public policies bearing on it have also changed. These developments give rise to new or renewed uncertainties among those exposed to social risk, that stretch well beyond the present contingencies. In addition to class risks, a second set of risks, in part new in themselves, in part the object of a new level of consciousness, distinguish themselves for their capacity to disorient us. They reflect globalisation, migrations, the growing need for depleted natural resources, the ecological costs that accompany them, the new but risky frontiers of biotechnologies, demographic growth and, last but not least, global warming. All these sources of risk touch on the sustainability of the human enterprise itself. The risk literature often tends to treat together the two broad categories of risk, as examples of the acceleration accumulation and temporal expansion of uncertainties, and as the wretched product of novel human ambitions ('manufactured risks'). Beck argues that the modern 'Fordist system', calibrated on the production and distribution of social goods, is being replaced by a postmodern risk regime in which 'social bads' prevail, affecting work security and safety but in addition, and more worryingly, our planet's sustainability (Beck 1998: 67–68).

In Chapter Seven, I will move my attention to this second type of risks. Now, in view of the emphasis I have given it so far, I will resume my treatment of social risks. I will examine what is commonly referred to as the privatisation of risk, its policies and its costs in terms of social cohesion. I speak of costs as losses, and losses in a double sense. The social policies of the past aimed at providing goods and services of social relevance. But they were also means or factors with a larger impact on the cohesion of the served community, its identity and its capacity to act. It is most clearly in regard to its attack on the policies of solidarity, and to its capacity to reverse the long-standing record of the modern state in dealing collectively with territory and population, that neoliberalism reveals its intimately

---

7. There are risks that, even if dealt with by, or in favour of, only one person, will necessarily benefit others. It may happen in the case of public or collective goods/services. For example, a mayor who is handicapped has the city add a bus stop in front of her residence. Her neighbours will also enjoy the service (free riders twice, as it were).

subversive perspectives. In comparison, as I shall show in Chapter Seven, the approach taken by neoliberal governments in regard to what I called above the second type of risks, the risks associated with what Jonas (1973) calls the boundless scope of human action, lacks the glue of a confident deontology, and is often characterised by contingent and opportunistic calculations of subjectively, and indeed conveniently, measured risks and costs.

The individualisation of social risk: government at a distance

A series of objective developments are unquestionably at the root of today's social risks. We have been witnessing irreversible transformations in the world of organised labour which impinge on the ways of being of an industrial and indeed industrious society, as they have been known and practiced until recent times. There are good reasons why we should reflect on the import of these transformations as something more than tinkering adjustments, recurring anomalies at most, bumps in an industrial trajectory that is otherwise linear and consequential.

We may think that, as serious as the task of understanding the new social risks and dealing with their impact on the world of work is, its dilemmas and uncertainties do not compare with those that accompany the risks of what I just referred to as the now boundless scope of human action. But it is a meager consolation. Neoliberalism, at any rate, has no need to decide what is more urgent, having already addressed the new social risks with verve and without uncertainties. Its blueprint is clear; it is constructed on a new, strongly reductive claim about the tasks of the state, in particular those concerning the governing of the social. I will look at the blueprint with particular reference to the United States and the United Kingdom, even though neoliberalism has a wide reach in the industrial world, wider than might transpire here. With its blueprint, neoliberalism is intervening in socioeconomic realities already undergoing transformation. The transformations alone do not explain the nature of neoliberal interventions. The latter are not a logical, necessary, direct or intuitive response, and certainly not the only possible ones, to the transformations. The question that I wish to address is therefore twofold: why those particular interventions?; and also, how and with what consequences do they influence the realities they step into? I called the neoliberal vision subversive in the literal sense of the word, in that, as stated, the conducts and the morals it wishes to impose on the individual are not only a retreat from the government of the social but also, and more tellingly (despite claims and appearances), the exact opposite of a return to the night-watchman myth of past liberal governments. Neoliberalism is no gentle return to minimal government: secular, liberal and only attentive, like the prudent physician conscious of his fallibility, to do no damage to his patients by excessive zeal.

Neoliberal intervention on the ongoing transformations in the world of work and production has produced an increase in those very uncertainties and insecurities and their associated costs, spilling into family and community structures already affected by those transformations. Widespread uncertainties are not unanticipated consequences of unfortunate policy miscalculations but the authentic outcome of the way in which neoliberalism problematises social risk. Its policies in regard to social risk reflect distrust toward the old instruments of public intervention, distrust in their material effectiveness and, principally, distrust in their ideal appropriateness. Social risk is no longer recognised as class risk and therefore loses the coverage and security guaranteed by twentieth century solidarity. The new policies aim at decoupling the protective pairing of safety with solidarity and at transferring on the individual the moral and financial burden of protection from risk. By directly addressing the individual and its conduct, neoliberalism intends to revive a presumably lost ethic of individual discipline and responsibility, obviously driven by a superior devotion to the public interest. In the neoliberal gospel, the virtues of the revival are both financial and moral.

In reality, few are in the position to personally bear the costs of social risk. In fact, few are in the position to know how to go about bearing the costs. To top it all, few are in the position to calculate with some comfort their long-term returns. Before discussing how the social policies of neoliberalism are responsible for these three incapacitations, I must place the discussion in the context of the new world of work and production, a world that, because of its troubling transformations, makes it more difficult for its subjects to assume personal charge of social risks. If the burden is accepted, it is frequently accepted under duress: the alternatives appear much more anguishing. The transformations are not transformations *in* the world of labour, perhaps temporary snags or well-meant tuning endeavours; they are transformations *of* the world of labour. Among them are deindustrialisation, exponential growth of the service sector, automation, the information revolution, new technologies and new professional requirements, job outsourcing, job insecurity and temporary employment, fragmentation and instability of the job market, all of them capped by a fall in unionisation and union resources in the private sector. Unavoidably, they impact work opportunities, work style and family life. Taken together and placed in perspective, they fit uncomfortably within last century's Fordist model. They are actually intimations of its ongoing subversion. This is the case because the Fordist model in *toto* was more than an industrial model affecting ways of production and ways of working. It was a much broader *tout se tient*, sufficiently protected from obsolescence over time. A whole series of systemic disciplines, threads of a warp now unraveling, have been part of a model within which the citizen-worker conducted himself in predictable fashion. Here is a long but partial list of those disciplines (some of the items in the list may precede early industrialisation but acquire weight with it): stable occupations professionally specified and covering the span of a work life; full-time full employment; predictable occupational hierarchies and careers; work as personal formation and identity; retirement as largely an actuarial fact; standardised mass production in large productive units; assigned work and rest schedules; natural resources intensively and extensively employed for productive purposes (nature at man's service); basic compulsory education; generational hierarchies; unity of the family nucleus; clear assignment of tasks and activities within the family; spare time as a break in the norm of work; social mobility between clearly defined social classes. To this list of systemic conducts we must add, especially relevant in Europe, the legislation and the policies that cemented and accredited them: collective bargaining; government sponsored *concertation sociale* embracing more than employment and labour conditions; codetermination; vertical concentration of labour and corporate interests; social market economy in the interest of private and social constituencies; progressive taxation; and, to close with Lipset, mass democracy supported by its commitment to wellbeing and solidarity.

It might be objected that this *tout se tient* picture is exceedingly ideal, as things did not go linearly and precisely as presented. For example, factory work was originally, and for a long period, part-time and seasonal, halfway between city and countryside (workers/peasants). Many workers, especially women and especially in the textile industry, worked from home. In the United States, the first social legislation did not cover industrial workers, it covered Civil War veterans and the families of soldiers who had died during that war (Skocpol 1992). Still, while the ideal model of the work society does not and cannot fully capture its necessarily non-linear genesis, it does describe its mature form. It therefore remains the starting point in the analysis of transformations past maturity.

Compared to the relatively stable composition of the labour force under the Fordist model, some of today's new labour sectors suffer under forms of employment exhibiting growing fluctuations and insecurity. This is the case of those employed in the new commercial and consumer services, such as super- and hyper-markets, fast food outlets, call centres, and national and international delivery systems. A similar predicament affects the sector of private or public assistance to old or disabled people, to single-parent or double-employment large families (care-givers, retirement home staff, nursery and kindergarten assistants, nannies, family workers). I also have in mind unstable employment in commercial sectors sensitive, in consumerist economies, to fluctuations in fashion and taste, often artificially driven by marketing campaigns. Fluctuation also threatens employees of more traditional commercial sectors, such as small, often family businesses, whose owners may not be able to deal with the competition of large business concentrations in the same sector. These and other service providers are essential for meeting the increasing request of personal and professional services (I add to the list the exclusive services to which the super-rich anxiously feel nowadays entitled). They are essential to sustain economies in which consumer spending for private goods and services plays an increasing role. These providers are physically everywhere, physically always present. They offer service schedules that go well beyond the 9 am to 5 pm, five-days-a-week, routine. Yet, they are also 'invisible' or, in the case of recent immigrants, they are forced to hide. In addition, they are poorly paid, poorly protected in aspects of life that go beyond their work, and more often than not they are non-unionised and discouraged from unionising. Other occupations to add to the list are hired security guards, parking attendants, doormen, gardeners, shop assistants, caterers, tellers, home delivery workers, and more.

We should not leave out, when it comes to the uncertainties of employment, professional sectors of high technological innovation, where high mobility and (possibly) high salaries may go together with high job and personal insecurity. We often praise work flexibility. But it is sufficient to distinguish, with Paolo

Ceri, between workers who are *flessibili* (flexible by choice) and workers who are *flessibilizzati* (forced into flexible jobs) to understand how different work opportunities are between, '[...] those who, because of the material and symbolic means[...] available to them, are in the position [...] to administer their flexibility and those who must place it in the hands of others ' (Ceri 2003: 80, my translation). Besides, even if *flessibili* workers have an advantage over *flessibilizzati*, their condition is not necessarily ideal when compared to a routinised past. On their new condition, Richard Sennett writes,

> In the revolt against routine, the appearance of a new freedom is deceptive. Time in institutions and for individuals has been unchained from the iron cage of the past, but subjected to new, top-down controls and surveillance. The time of flexibility is the time of a new power. Flexibility begets disorder, but not freedom from restraint. (Sennet 1998: 59)

In this sense, the very distinction between *flessibili* and *flessibilizzati* becomes opaque, both in terms of their respective capacities to pursue the kind of job they seek, and in terms of the respective flexibility of the jobs they end up with.

These final observations about occupational flexibility also apply quite well to what is left of the Fordist system. In it, we witness the expansion of production methods emphasising new flexibility in the productive cycle and the circulation of knowledge and occupations. It follows that even within the Fordist system there is no longer guarantee of remuneration levels or job security, no longer guarantee of collective covering, present or over time, of health and pension coverage, especially for new employees. It follows in turn that, when a job is insecure, unstable, and/or part-time, when working hours fluctuate with the new flexibility of production cycles and demands, and when the workers or members of their family remedy all of this by taking additional jobs, then past opportunities for community dwindle, family life is disrupted, and free time is not only limited, it is also time alone ('bowling alone?'). Sennett's book, cited above, is in essence an analysis of how flexibility, even when it comes to the most privileged occupations, impacts affected workers not only objectively but also subjectively. The title of his book is *The Corrosion of Character: The personal consequences of work in the New Capitalism*. I may be misinterpreting the author but I would summarise his message as follows: a worker's sense of responsibility toward co-workers is obviously a function of one's opportunity to enter into a steady community of work. Without that opportunity, the flexible worker rationalises isolation. You are on your own. Sennett's corrosion of character under new forms of work is the corrosion of personal responsibility.

I move briefly to the strictly economic costs, borne especially by the common people, which accompany the epochal transformations in the world of occupation and production. One concrete example comes from the paragraph where I mentioned the workers' waning guarantees within what remains of the Fordist system. Some of the reasons for diminishing guarantees lie outside the flexibilisation of the productive system. They lie with the broader neoliberal climate and the broader transformations outside the Fordist model. Both of them induce 'Fordist' employers, rationally in a way, to weaken the traditional guarantees they are burdened with. Given that neoliberalism preaches that each citizen is to be individually responsible for his choices, of which he should carry the weight and consequences; given that the removal of collective entitlements as morally corrupting and fiscally irresponsible should be (as a minimum) a government's default position; given, in addition, that the workforce outside the Fordist system is already much less protected from social risk, why then should we be surprised if Fordist employers try to get themselves a better deal? After all, they have often carried a significant part of the entitlement burden, as is the case of the costly pension funds covering America's automobile workers. And since public control on the respect of labour legislation in the sector is haphazard and declining, why not take advantage, as documented by Steven Greenhouse (2008), of the opportunity?

Here are samples of the economic costs that common people bear. Peter Gosselin collected and presented data showing that, from the middle of the seventies to the early years of the new millennium (that is, before the 2008 economic recession), the percentage of families experiencing the kind of family events that may cause financial volatility – loss of a job, sickness, disability, retirement, death, divorce, even a birth – has not changed (if at all, it has slightly declined) (Gosselin 2008). It was and remains around 20 per cent. However, almost twice as many of those families have seen their annual income cut in half (from 5 to 9 per cent). It means that those changes in family life are now much more likely to wreck a family. True, on the whole the percentage is still small. However, Gosselin adds data showing that the incomes of families who have not experienced those changes are also experiencing mainly downward income volatility. This is particularly the case for poorer or less educated families, as well as younger families. They are precisely the families most likely to experience greater trouble if any of those events materialise. Gosselin has good reasons to suggest that the growth in the number of families experiencing financial instability reflects the weakening of the social safety nets under neoliberal administrations – a weakening that is capable of financially eroding not only family income and income security, but also family assets and other measures of total wealth. Jeff Madrick's data and analysis (Madrick 2009) are on the same wavelength as Gosselin's. A series of data covering the last four decades of American economic and labour history documents two of the most recent developments: the stagnation of the American economy and, in parallel, the declining life standards of the average American family.

These are only two among many more studies that, especially after the economic recession, have delved into the predicament of America's other half, or, shall we say, the other 99 per cent. Dealing with various aspects of average America's social predicament, they converge on a broader picture of that predicament. But my intent is not to present a quantitative analysis, which other researchers are better equipped to present; my intent is to examine the political and policy concomitants and components of this predicament. Further, the United States may offer the most macroscopic and ideal-typical picture, but many of the predicaments are shared by other advanced democracies. I will only stress one feature that the analysts of these predicaments share. Although some are political scientists and many more are economists, all of them put a special emphasis on politics and policies. This is not so surprising when it comes to political scientists and sociologists; it is refreshingly surprising with economists. Traditionally, self-assured economists have sought explanations in their own realm. They have gone after macroscopic variables such as globalisation (an easy *passe-partout*), trade, and technologies; they have gone after presumably unassailable classical economic modelling. But some of them have recently discovered that these variables do not travel far.[8]

I shall now move to the contribution that neoliberal politics and policies make to the predicaments above. I start by placing the discussion in the broader context of the popular attraction that the neoliberal narrative intends to elicit, as it emphasises the freedom and equality of a consumer society and a consuming citizen. To announce, in a sort of morality play, that we are all, or shall and should be, middle class (a homogenising term that even critics of neoliberalism mindlessly employ), is to try and mentally remove the main source of our collective identities under industrial society, i.e. our occupations, the contribution they made to our communities, and the attention they received by our governments. It means to reset our life conditions; now measured with the metro of ownership and displayed in shared consumptions and material desires. It means to announce that class hierarchies mediated by solidarity no longer describe us and no longer have reasons to exist. Now, with the wave of a wand, class hierarchies give way to a project of equality that relies on consumption open to all. In addition, consumption becomes a surreptitious synonym of freedom. However, the equations do not add up, not when it comes to being and feeling equal, and certainly not when it comes to being and feeling free. Equality *de facto* cannot be measured in terms of consumption accessible to all. Minimally, equality must be measured in terms of the personal and collective resources on which we rely. This way of measuring reveals that, even if we live in societies that are relatively affluent and seduced by consumption, inequalities in terms of income, wealth and much more (including how much and what we consume) have steadily and strongly increased. The general evidence for the last thirty or forty years clearly shows income and wealth stagnation for almost all citizens, and a formidable progressive increase, despite the 2008 recession, in the income and wealth of those who occupy the very top of the earning ladder. Further, the growth in how much a given amount of money can buy is not linear. As earners move toward the top, their capacity to buy more is not limited to ordinary goods and services; to more but more of the same. The super-rich can buy influence, access, public recognition for the civic generosity they alone can afford, unique services, priority protection, exclusive entitlements

---

8. I mention the latest work of two distinguished economists, Joseph Stiglitz (2012) and Paul Krugman (2012) and one newspaper editor Hedrick Smith (2012). All three document the devastating effects of recent neoliberal policies on the American economy in general and on the wellbeing of large strata of the populations, the bottom strata in particular. All three insist on the limits of macroeconomic explanations.

and tax shelters; all of which other earners, even relatively affluent ones, cannot buy. The super-rich can also buy things that, as Michael Sandel puts it, money should not buy.[9]

As inequalities have grown, their growth is not simply due to spontaneous national and global macroeconomic processes. Growth coincides with neoliberal policies aimed on the one hand at curtailing the only collective resource of those in need, i.e. their social entitlements, and at supporting supposedly virtuous investors by means, for instance, of appropriate fiscal policies and other corporate entitlements. Whether they actually invest, and with what benefits for society and the economy at large, is, as well documented, a totally different story. But there lies the cultural lure of the narrative. And there, also, lies the politically legitimated temptation of the American super-rich to finally think of themselves as a deservingly separate class, entitled to special treatment. One of the super-rich (who will remain anonymous)[10] declares, 'you'd rather have control of the money than the government [...] Even if you're giving it away, you'd rather give it away the way you want.' Another of the super-rich explains, 'People don't realise how wealthy people self-tax [...] If you have a certain cause, an art museum or a symphony, and you want to support it, it would be nice if you had the choice'. Needless to say, but also besides the point, donations are tax-exempt. Another factor spurring the super-rich to protect their riches is the special importance we all assign to losing what we already have (an example of so-called loss aversion). The rich, in principle, have a lot to lose; the poor, in fact, have little or nothing to lose. As Jeffrey Winters writes, '[...] poverty by itself neither motivates nor provides a core set of common interests for the poor the way wealth does for the rich [...] Wealth is inherently empowering and motivating, poverty is neither' (Winters 2011: 5).

The super-rich cited above are not the self-effacing Weberian practitioners of nascent capitalism; they do not practice Montesquieu's *doux commerce*; they are not the bleak utilitarians of Dickens' novels; they are not frugal Boston Brahmins, nor are they first-generation Buddenbrooks; nor even the titans of early American capitalism. They are the self-proclaimed master-race of newfangled turbo-capitalism (assuming that capitalism is still the best description). Not quite two hundred years ago, Alexis de Tocqueville intuited with extraordinary foresight the special status of the very rich, in the closing chapter of *Democracy in America*'s second part, second book, (Ch. 20). His foresight is the more remarkable as Tocqueville could not possibly anticipate either the new productive sources of national wealth, or the political contribution of neoliberalism to the

---

9.   Sandel writes, 'The more money can buy, the more affluence (or the lack of it) matters. If the only advantage of affluence were the ability to buy yachts, sports cars, and fancy vacations, inequalities of income and wealth would not matter very much. But as money comes to buy more and more [...] the distribution of income and wealth looms larger and larger' (Sandel 2012: 8).

10. His identity, as that of the other super-rich cited in the text, is available in Christia Freeland, *Super-rich Irony, New Yorker*, 8 October 2012: 44–51. Both citations are on p.48.

erosion of democratic equality. While America struck him as quintessentially and uniquely marked by equality of conditions, and the rich as largely devoid of collective purposes, ambitions and identities of their own, he also contemplated the distinct possibility of an end to that happy state. The chapter, a masterful analysis of unanticipated consequences, is worth reading in its entirety. It starts by foreseeing the equalising benefits that successful mass production for mass consumption will bring about under democracy, and ends with an intuition of the equivalent of neoliberal neglect of inequality. Mass production will benefit mass consumption, but will also financially benefit the producers and strengthen their class identification. The title of the chapter is 'How an aristocracy may be created by manufactures'. Mass production and consumption will benefit those who produce them because,

> As the conditions of men [...] become more and more equal, the demand for more manufactured commodities becomes more general and extensive [...] Hence there are every day more men of great opulence and education who devote their wealth and knowledge to manufactures and who seek [...] to meet the fresh demands [...] Thus, in proportion as the mass of the nation turns to democracy, that particular class which is engaged in manufactures becomes more aristocratic [...] The small aristocratic societies that are formed by some manufacturers in the midst of the immense democracy of our age contain [...] some men who are very opulent and a multitude who are wretchedly poor. The poor have few means of escaping [...]. (Tocqueville [1840] 1994: Pt.2, Bk.II: 159–60)

If so, Tocqueville continues,

> I am of the opinion, on the whole, that the manufacturing aristocracy which is growing up under our eyes is one of the harshest that ever existed in the world; but at the same time it is one of the most confined and least dangerous. Nevertheless, the friends of democracy should keep their eyes anxiously fixed in this direction; for if ever a permanent inequality of conditions and aristocracy again penetrates into the world, it may be predicted that this is the gate by which they will enter. (Tocqueville [1840] 1994: Pt.2, Bk.II: 161)

So much for 'actual' equality, whether it is equality under Tocqueville's mass manufacturing, when workers were not yet protected, or equality under neoliberalism today, when workers stand to lose their protection.

As to feeling equal, in Western societies where a degree of average wellbeing is accompanied by considerable inequalities, the feeling, when present, constitutes, to use a well-worn trope, false consciousness. It may give us illusory comfort if – a necessary but at present improbable condition – expectations of average wellbeing endure. Further, those who enjoy false consciousness, false because heedless, are likely to personally bear its unfortunate consequences. One factor that feeds false consciousness is the siren of easy access to cheap consumption open to everyone. The siren is nourished by the standardisation of mass supply; by the artificial levelling of taste resulting from vicarious gratifications for all (cheap imitations of luxury goods, exotic vacation packages); and by the competitive individualisation of the consumer and his cravings. Sermonising analysts may take pleasure in dissecting the immoral qualities of these sirens. But, in so doing, they (indeed we) also risk overlooking that many consumptions are neither voluptuary nor affordable. I am thinking in particular of incumbent necessities (health, assistance, education) the costs of which many in need cannot carry. Furthermore, we once lived under the joint auspices of citizenship and solidarity,[11] where solidarity made the *demos* all-inclusive and gave meaning to citizenship. We are now invited to live as consumers, where consumer should pair with citizen. But consumption does not make the citizen. The pairing makes no sense, except by extravagant definition. More importantly, for those who, propelled by market fetishism, may still embrace the pairing, the revelation that what they can afford to consume is not on a par may, ironically, clip their very sense of being citizens.

As to being or feeling free, the facts in the above paragraph are reason for scepticism. Strange is the freedom that comes to us from our individual engagement in the market and its allegedly lifting effects. It is strange, but also off the mark, because the freedoms we know and rely on are the freedoms that go with political rights. They are a sort of collective good: the essence of citizenship. Freedom that comes from the market is also a false freedom, for two reasons. First, as I have just shown, equal access to the market is only an enticing fiction. Second, freedom under the market, as theorised and promised by neoliberalism, is not a natural condition, which we would spontaneously revert to once the artifice of government is removed. On the contrary, neoliberal policies are needed that force us (do as I say, or else...) to seek neoliberal freedom and embrace a new beginning. To spur us toward the new beginning, neoliberal governments systematically employ a series of disciplinary techniques intended to make us free and self-reliant, for our own and everybody's good. Actual constriction, in the form of the higher costs of doing otherwise is papered over by a moralising tale about the miraculous power

---

11. Some of the new needs are not fancies; objective developments are making them material necessities. Many workers are compelled to rely for professional reasons on the new information technologies, in particular, personal computers. In some cases the computer replaces the office, not only by preference and convenience. It allows, for the first time, some people to have an 'office' without the unbearable costs of a brick and mortar one. Once upon a time, we used pencils and pens, we then moved on to typewriters. Now, the former are auxiliary, the latter is in the attic or the museum. True, goods and services provided by the informatics revolution are progressively more accessible. But, again, for many, these goods and services are not a luxury. Today, a college education is less and less a path to elite formation, more and more the extremely costly training that is necessary (if not always sufficient in the present economic turmoil) in order to fit into the world of work. In the Fordist system, a certificate of vocational training offered ample opportunities of comfortable employment. Therefore, to argue, for instance, that because more people have college degrees, professional and life standards have improved, is to miss the point entirely. There has been an increase in professional requirements and standards, but the increase, inescapable as it is, is no synonym of professional and life improvement. In addition, for the many that are left behind there loom the increasing prospects of professional debasement and socioeconomic inequalities.

of spontaneous self-reliance and responsibility.

Hacker *et al.* comment, acerbically,

> Even as the new political order stresses individual liberties [...] government has adopted a more muscular, directive stance toward the poor, particularly the nonwhite poor. For these groups, the American state has become more directive, custodial and punitive [...]. In the mid-twentieth century, disadvantaged Americans came to experience government as a source of economic security and opportunity. Today [...]. (Soss *et al.* 2007: 19)

Here, adjectives like 'muscular', 'punitive', and 'custodial' instinctively echo Foucault's discipline in the classical modern state. But there is something collective about Foucault's discipline that sets it apart from individualised neoliberal discipline. In regard to discipline and the individual dependency that accompanies it, Foucault recognises two types of dependency, with two different effects, 'an effect of dependency by integration and an effect of dependency by marginalisation or exclusion' (in Kritzman 1988: 163).[12] By stressing the communal effect of discipline, the former dependency echoes Mary Douglas and Louis Dumont's inclusive hierarchy in the modern state. What makes the latter dependency less inviting is the fact that it relies on a perversely promising neoliberal premise: that the market, being a fact of nature, is sufficient to give birth to a citizen/consumer who benefits economically, hence politically, the community by benefitting himself. I speak of the neoliberal premise as perverse in the sense in which Albert Hirschman (1991: ch.2) uses the adjective when describing one of the consequences that reactionaries attach to reform policies. I intend to take apart the premise and its consequences by degrees.

I start with a first, rhetorical, question. Is a market that is freed from the artificial state the proper arena to forge an economy that benefits all by benefitting the few that drive it? If the answer were yes, it might suggest that the market is, after all, not only efficient but also a significant sponsor of civic responsibility. I am using an admittedly special case to answer the question with a 'no'. The case is special not because it is surprising. It is exceptional in scale, but it is not an exception, a fluke within an otherwise responsible economy. I am referring to the 2008 economic recession with its lingering economic consequences and to the beliefs and behaviours that preceded, accompanied and followed it. The recession was sustained, though not singly caused, by a misplaced faith in the self-corrective wisdom of a market that was presumably prospering because it was free of external controls and regulations. This faith has long been buttressed among policy makers, often irrespective of their partisan collocations, by the unchallenged domain, in academia and think tanks, of classical and neo-classical economic theories, often conveniently stretched. Incidentally, the stretching obscures, intentionally or not, the actual differences, political and economic, between classical liberalism and neoliberalism. Be as it may, long before the recession, those theories had displaced,

---

12. The conclusions I draw are mine. I am not claiming Foucauldian support for them.

in academia and in the economic world, among experts and political advisers, Keynesian economics. In addition, the economic euphoria preceding the recession and the expansionist bubbles that went with it, had been especially nurtured by the aggressive innovations, deregulation, and growing weight of financial markets. Investors, experts and policy makers have discounted, minimised or, in the light of greater actual or expected returns, downright welcomed the greater risks and fluctuations associated with the greater unpredictability of these markets. A market that encourages euphoric, even fraudulent, behaviour encourages precisely the opposite of much-acclaimed individual responsibilities. After the recession, many, but not all,[13] have come to recognise the subjective reasons (misplaced trust in the market, occasionally fraudulence) why things went wrong. There was no lack of warning signs, but like voices in the desert they went unheard.

Undoubtedly, euphoria has been supported, and perhaps driven, by the cultural climate of so-called turbo-capitalism or, to bring the euphoria down to the professional investors, by the psychology that infuses what Bennett Harrison called impatient capital, i.e. capital in search of quick, high returns (Harrison 1994: 214). Personal euphoria is compounded by deep-lying individual dispositions. As with gambling, so also with impatient capital: if it delivers despite the risks, why give up before it is too late? Subjectively, what will make late too late? A case in point, explored recently by neuro-economics (Zweig 2007),[14] is the trust that successful market operators place in the continuity of their success. This is the type of trust that finally fed into the global crisis of the financial system. Neuro-economics experiments show that trust in the endurance of success is greater if success has come despite high risks. In addition, in the case of the financial bubbles, the incentive to continue risky behaviour came from the fact that the risks

---

13. Philip Mirowski, historian and economic philosopher, has written a short essay (Mirowski 2010) offering a psychological explanation, tolerant in a way, for enduring deafness. According to Mirowski, the refusal of quite a number of orthodox economists to recognise where they went wrong is a textbook case of cognitive dissonance. If the evidence does not confirm but actually overturns prophecies, creeds and expectations, it is because something is wrong with the evidence. After all, the formal modelling that neoclassical economics practices, its emphasis on positive choice, cannot go wrong. But, Mirowski asks, is it really science? Better, is it necessary in order to do right, that we have a science? Since it is not necessary, then those who claim otherwise are living a scientific illusion; they stick to a creed that should be tottering. But why shouldn't they? As long as it delivered, it proved that the accounting offered by positive choice theory was simplicity itself. And if evidence shows that it delivers no longer, something is the matter with the data. Some of these points are treated in the volume on the postwar theoretical roots of neoliberalism edited by Mirowski and Plehwe (2011).

14. Already, in 1936, Keynes saw in the impulsiveness of what he called 'animal spirits' a hazard factor in economic fluctuations, as such needing guidance and control. On animal spirits he wrote, 'Most [...] of our decisions to do something positive, the full consequences of which will be drawn out over many days to come, can only be taken as the result of animal spirits – a spontaneous urge to action rather than inaction, and not as the outcome of a weighted average of quantitative benefits multiplied by quantitative probabilities' (Keynes 1936: 161–62). Needless to say, even among his followers, his warning fell on deaf ears. The warning was *ante litteram. Animal Spirits* is today the title of a book by George Akerlof and Robert Shiller (2009), subtitled, *How Human Psychology Drives the Economy and why it Matters for Global Capitalism.*

were dumped on unknown others. The more the risks of investing and lending were dispersed and parcelled-out, the less were the personal and corporate risks of investors and lenders. Help came in recent times from public policies aimed at stimulating presumably risk-free financial behaviour by expressly removing burdensome regulations and shielding the personal returns of financial operators from the consequences of reckless operations. The chimera of growth and easy profit, free of public control, tells us to invest with cockiness. Risk and the future are discounted. We take it erroneously for granted that market contexts and the nature of risk stay the same. We are confident that success will accompany us, even if new unforeseen risks border on sheer gambling. I am strong therefore I am lucky. On 28 March 2003, Jimmy Cayne, CEO of Bear Sterns, told a *New York Times* journalist,

> What can we do better? [...] I just can't decide what that might be [...] Everyone says that when the markets turn around, we will suffer. But let me tell you, we are going to surprise some people this time around. Bear Sterns is a great place to be.

Was this a case of almightiness (the stronger the enemy, the bigger the victory), blindness, or superstition? Bear Sterns, once a great place, is no longer a place at all.[15] Another reason for misplaced confidence in the market is the drive to compete that lies inside new, high-flying lucrative professions. The need to prove one's status and worth is an inducement to keep up with the booming successes of one's colleagues. And avidity by demonstration-effect may slide, as it did with the recession, into the corruption of the market and the malfeasance of some of its operators.

And there is more. The promise of investing without risk did not entice professional investors only; sadly, it enticed on their coat-tails myriads of ordinary consumers. Their majority was made of less affluent people, not particularly versed in the games and tricks of artificial wealth. Enticing stock options in a buoyant stock market, a booming housing market, deceivingly easy loans and mortgages, credit cards, deferred payments, easy refinancing; all of these devices artificially stretch the catalogue of presumptive human needs, from what is apparently available to what is desirable, and from what is desirable to what is deemed necessary. With one difference, that once the recession hits, the professional investors may lose, by and large, only part of their investments, thanks also to emergency rescue legislation. But the ordinary consumers may lose their shirt and more. They are the first and maybe only ones who, untutored and deprived of tangible coverage and other resources, are left carrying the real burden of a dysfunctional market in which they trusted.

---

15. But the costs of its malfeasance, borne by investors in the bank's mortgage securities, linger on. They brought about, in October 2012, an indictment by the Attorney General of the state of New York.

So we meet once again a double standard. It is to the ordinary people that I now return; to their negative experiences when it comes to risk, to the promise, false or betrayed that it might be, of an individualising emancipation from the ground up. To individualise risk boils down to denying, materially and normatively, its collective nature. It means to deny the support, often implicit, which it finds in reciprocal trust or minimally in reciprocal tolerance. Thus, risk is no longer part of all of us together and, so to say, outside the singleton and his/her burdens. In the neoliberal narrative, risk coverage can never be the default position; on the contrary, it is a position to be avoided at all costs. Risk coverage is best conceived of as an individual duty, for which each upright consumer responsibly pays. It quickly follows that those who are at risk and can pay will take care of themselves. And the fact that they are able to pay will prove in their mind that they are responsible citizens. It is not surprising if they are induced to see themselves as virtuous, different from 'the others'. It is not surprising if individualising risk ends up by inducing the virtuous ones to judge, classify, stereotype, stigmatise, fear and ultimately exclude 'the others'. We might point out that the virtuous ones are simply more fortunate. But even their own fortune may have limits. At times, personal assumption of risk, even on the part of the most willing and informed, may not pay off. [16] And if some of the self-styled virtuous were not to feel rewarded, because they still feel at risk but have difficulties in reconstructing why, a way out is for them to dump their resentment on others.[17] Resentment employs moralising categories that give comfort to the moraliser by belittling the vicious circle of adversities under which the rest of us, 'the others', live.[18] Disdain removes the fact that 'the others' are usually concentrated in demographic groups naturally exposed to greater risks, less endowed with material and psychological defences, and therefore more easily overwhelmed by the risks' full impact. The predicament besetting 'the others' alerts us to the falseness of the neoliberal public creed; namely, that entrusting people with the care of themselves will leave

---

16. Consider the case of the American health system. Until the recent reform sponsored by President Obama, and still contested as socialised medicine even though it remains a largely privatised system, the American health system was marked by the pursuit of profit by insurers, fees for services, preferential coverage of the healthier ones, plus deregulation, high fragmentation, and dispersion of the insurance and reinsurance markets. These are all features that make the system especially difficult to navigate, even for the more informed.

17. An extensive treatment of this source of social resentment is in Young (2007).

18. As an everyday example, I cite a 1 August 2008 report by National Public Radio. NPR reported that day that a high percentage of the Latino population affected by intestinal cancer has a lower chance of survival in respect to the general population of intestinal cancer patients. This is because their cancer is detected at an advanced stage. Why? Because, and I cite, 'for cultural reasons' Latinos go to the doctor only when they are very sick. This is to suggest that being late is their fault, as it must also be the fault of other categories that defer treatment until forced to visit emergency rooms. This in turn unquestionably and considerably increases the costs of the American health system. I cited NPR because of the deservedly high prestige of the network and because of its generally 'liberal' orientation.

them economically and morally better, as well as free at last to pursue happiness. Formulated for public consumption, the creed takes for granted the implausible: i.e. a uniformly persuasive internalisation of its message. It shows indifference, indeed insensitivity, toward everything that puts uniform internalisation into question, be it group identities, resources, knowledge, beliefs, values or aimless instinctive reactions.

The climate of induced suspicion toward the others-than-us may reach the absurd. Witness the unconscionable ordinance, adopted on 19 July 2006, by the city council of Las Vegas (of all places). The ordinance imposed severe fines and possible incarceration on anybody who, in a public park, offered 'free of charge or for a nominal sum, food to an indigent'. It defined as indigent somebody who an ordinary person reasonably believes to have title to receive or apply for public assistance. This gives rise to two possible scenarios. An 'ordinary' person will still be able to share his picnic with an occasional indigent, provided the indigent is well-dressed or distinguished by other signs of apparent wellbeing. Alternatively, the ordinary person may improvise, and convince the cop that is going to fine him that the person he intends to feed may well look shabby, but shabbiness, in his opinion as an upright citizen, does not give title to public assistance; ergo, in his view as an ordinarily reasonable person, the shabby person in question is not an indigent, hence he is going to feed him. Was the city council of Las Vegas, the capital of entertainment, showing its sense of humour, or was it utterly devoid of one?[19]

---

19. Unexceptional in comparison is the attitude of the city lawyer of St. Petersburg (Fla) who, in homage perhaps to Anatole France's famous dictum, Solomonically declared (June 2009), 'Whether you are millionaire or homeless, if you stretch yourself on the sidewalk, you are in violation of the city ordinance'. Except that France's dictum was intended as unmitigated sarcasm.

Chapter Five

Toward the Criminalisation of the Other

In this chapter I continue the analysis of neoliberal policies toward class risks. I focus at greater length on three aspects. First, the policies require and seek intrusive micromanagement that belies government at a distance driven by the automatisms of the market. In the second place, the policies contribute to the disorganisation of the community as a whole. The sociabilities of the public sphere come apart and their organising structures withdraw into themselves, often in irreversible manners. A 'positive feedback' process is activated that advances by feeding on itself (Pierson 2004). Finally, the marginalisation of the others turns into increasing criminalisation; this, with the help of a novel post-welfare construction of criminal law as punitive, confining and preventive (the criminal as predictably habitual predator).

A parody of *laissez faire*

Never in the history of liberal democracies has the market of exchange of goods and services single-handedly and spontaneously shaped, let alone subjected and defined, the public sphere where civil society and government converge. The equation is simply untenable. The economic market can never be, has never been and never will be the prime and only mover. This is not to deny that the market in the context of a liberal-democratic state has been one of the models molding the exchange practices of the public sphere and one of the 'positive feedback' factors in structuring its actions. Nor do I mean to deny that market stakeholders have legitimate claims in democratic politics, just like workers, just like other interests and opinions. However, these normal aspects of market economies in democratic politics have nothing whatsoever to do with the absurd idea that a quintessential democracy is one in which politics *is* market-like and only market-like. They have nothing to do with the belief that every aspect of individual and public life should be and can be conflated into market-like rationality. However, neoliberalism then enters and boldly, indeed magically, denies the impossible, and attends to prove itself right. If, today, a specious idea of politics as market has insinuated itself, redefining the past practices and the structuring of the public sphere, this is because of the concerted actions and claims of neoliberal governments. Thus the logic of the market has come to affect the conduct of government in areas of collective public action that had previously nothing to do with private economies. These are areas where, as we shall see, the pursuit of government effectiveness is also narrowed to a presumably objective accounting of input-output market effectiveness. Finally, decisive for the cultural dominance of its narrative, neoliberalism buttresses its new style of government with the authority of an epochal reproblematisation. It does this by claiming the inherent total wisdom of the market, and by theorising a virtuous, hopefully seductive, system of governing at a distance as the most appropriate for the final fulfilment of a so-called market society. The seductive aspect of governing at a distance resides, for those at its receiving end, in the promise that, thanks to the energies it releases, individual citizens, with their primary groups and natural sociabilities, will be able, as they must, to take direct care of themselves, to protect themselves from risks, and, in sum, to govern themselves without the debilitating impediments of *the* government. Congratulations, you are on your own, you are your own master.

However, that announced distance, making people supposedly appreciative of a diminutive government, exists only as a fiction intended to seduce. In reality, the ideal order that neoliberalism announces does not and cannot spring from nor can it be sustained by the publicised fiction of a naturally free and levelled market in which individual parties spontaneously meet. Smithian sympathy and trust may help the parties. But Smithian dispositions occupy a moral space beyond the naked market calculations in which neoliberalism claims to confide. Besides, sympathy and trust are not sufficient. Further, neoliberalism is conscious of the fiction; or perhaps, more charitably, it suffers from a case of false consciousness. There are, in this regard, two neoliberal narratives. One is the simplifying, disarming narrative for public consumption, pithily captured by the already quoted statement, a perfect case of axiomatic thinking, contained in Ronald Reagan's inaugural address, 'In the present crisis government is not the solution to our problems; government is the problem'. The other is the narrative mostly reserved for the insiders. When it comes to the insiders, what they knowingly practice is what I glossed above as muscular, punitive, custodial government. Speaking of market fundamentalism, Somers and Block describe the politics underneath the double narrative as follows, '[…] market fundamentalism engages in a double talk – using ideational power to construct markets by means of draconian laws and policies, while simultaneously insisting that the process is entirely natural and a political' (Somers and Block 2005: 282–83). There are different explanations for the double talk. At times the explanations are competing, at times overlapping; at times they are offered by different authors, at times by the same ones.

The explanation that is most congenial to the assertors of neoliberalism's virtue is Malthusian: welfarism has slowly eroded the natural habits of self-reliance, the capacity and will to stand on one's own, thus producing the unsustainable opposite of what it aimed for. This is a good example of Albert Hirschman's already cited reactionary 'rhetoric of perversity' (Hirschman 1991: Ch.2). Exactly the same one-dimensional unbending rhetoric employed 150 years before by the English critics of the Poor Law, Hirschman argues, was used in the 1970s to denounce the effects of Lyndon Johnson's Great Society. The rhetoric of perversity, Hirschman shows, is more than a self-serving political ruse. It had, at the time, a strong intellectual pedigree in England; it acquired, in the aftermath of the Great Society, a strong academic pedigree in the United States. It follows, for those who still embrace the perversity thesis, that redressing perversity necessitates a programme of guided re-education that should recover individuals for the virtuous life of a catallactic order.[1] While other advocates of welfare reform are concerned with its running fiscal costs and their impact on growth, the neoliberal critique of welfare has deeper existential concerns. Transferring responsibility to the individual is at its core a question of inducing individuals, constructed by the neoliberal narrative as carriers as much as victims of social risks, to mend their ways ('welfare to work'). More broadly, it is a question of 'naturalising' society from the bottom up (Margaret Thatcher), by disciplining as necessary. Naturalising society is a superior end in itself, to achieve which both the individual and the state must reform themselves in market terms.

Another explanation for the double talk is more esoteric and academic. Neoliberalism does not actually believe in the spontaneity of the market. Rather, it moves from a profound ontological pessimism, as elaborated by early neoliberal think tanks such as the Mont Pélerin Society (Mirowski and Plehwe 2009: 417–56), about the existence in the individual of an innate capacity to fully wish and live in a catallactic order (Pellicani 2010: Ch.9). What is necessary is not re-education into mythical habits but education to the new, and this is the task of the state on behalf of the market.[2] Karl Polanyi captured this self-serving neoliberal enlistment of the state in his analysis of the sudden dominance of market economy in nineteenth century England,

> Actually [...] the behaviour of man both in his primitive state and right through the course of history has been almost the opposite of that implied in this view [...] [that the market would spontaneously arise, if only men were let alone] [...] On the contrary, the market has been the outcome of the conscious and often violent intervention on the part of government which imposed the market organisation on society *for noneconomic ends*. (Polanyi 1957: 257–58 [my emphasis]).

For Polanyi this was the story of a 'cataclysm' (Polanyi 1957: 4); for neoliberalism it was and remains a necessity, and an ongoing programme of government.[3]

---

1. The banal Malthusianism of this position is tersely captured in a March 2012 declaration by Paul Ryan, House Budget Committee Chairman and later Republican candidate to the vice-presidency. Commenting his proposed budgetary cuts to legal aid for the disabled, Ryan explained, 'We don't want to turn the safety net into a hammock that lulls able-bodied people into lives of dependency and complacency, that drains them of their will and their incentive to make the most of their lives'. Reported by Paul Krugman, *New York Times*, 24 August 2012.

2. For this purpose, neoliberal economists (Friedrich von Hayek, Milton Friedman) supported and offered guidance to Augusto Pinochet's authoritarian government. Friedman paid an official visit.

3. However, Polanyi also powerfully argued throughout his book that, as a utopia, the idea that a market economy could exist spontaneously, disembedded from society, or on society by government imposed, could not have a long life: 'Nineteenth Century [English] society in which economic activity was isolated and imputed to a distinctive economic motive, was, indeed, a singular departure' (Polanyi 1957: 71). The postwar notion of embedded liberalism as the normal condition under which a market economy could operate (Ruggie 1982) was borrowed from Polanyi.

A third explanation of neoliberal double-talk deepens the second one and involves a variation on both Bourdieu's 'from utopia to program' (1998) and on Somers and Block (2005). In effect, neoliberalism sells as solid reality what is programmatic advocacy. Wendy Brown explains,

> Neo-liberalism involves a normative rather than ontological claim about the pervasiveness of economic rationality and advocates the institution-building, policies, and discourse development appropriate to such a claim. Neo-liberalism is a constructivist project: it does not presume the ontological givenness of a thoroughgoing economic rationality for all domains of society but rather takes as its task the development, dissemination, and institutionalisation of such a rationality [...]

> The state is not without a project in the making of the neo-liberal subject. The state attempts to construct prudent subjects through policies that organise such prudence [...] Because neo-liberalism casts rational action as a norm rather than an ontology, social policy is the means by which the state produces subjects whose compass is set by their rational assessment of the costs and benefits of certain acts. (Brown 2003: 9, 16)

Whichever of the three explanation we embrace,[4] the conclusion is the same: Neoliberalism governs because its project requires that it governs. But it governs with a different face, one that, while governing, publicly exhibits distance, plus suspicion and distrust, in regard to government itself. Distance, suspicion and distrust actually go beyond government in the narrow sense of authoritative institutions. Equally, they dismiss civil society's discursive relations with public institutions. Thus, governing at a distance may sound liberating but it may also sound less comforting, like distanced government. In a context of social fragmentation, dispersion of action arenas and risk uncertainties, it sounds improvidently disengaging. An indication, but not a proof, of such feelings comes from a considerable fall, by opinion polls regularly documented, in trust in government and its efficient and accountable operation, accompanied by an increase in feelings that governments are remote and inscrutable. This rejection may strike some as puzzling. If the purpose of governing at a distance is to strengthen the hand of citizens as rightful consumers of services; if its purpose is to create an 'ownership society', so that unencumbered citizens can personally deal with risks and opportunities, why then should people be suspicious? Public reaction should tend toward the opposite: citizen and government should be in synch, their relations more personal; government's standing in regard to the citizen/consumer

---

4. There is what I consider a fourth reason. I would call it a by-reason as it stems from what may be charitably seen as an unforeseen consequence of the neoliberal pursuit of government at a distance. To anticipate, the presumed automatisms of the 'New Public Management' and the increasing use of market-oriented private-public partnerships carry with themselves an unprecedented degree of surveillance. Concretely, surveillance means auditing, administration and bureaucratisation. Another more assuasive name for these developments is new contractualism.

should be more tangible and transparent. All of this stands to reason except that it is up to the citizen to figure out how to engage. And if he cannot, it is at least an open question as to whether or not he will rightly hold himself responsible. Will he embrace the neoliberal 'tough-love' slogan or resent being instructed that he is on his own? I discussed above, speaking of the literature on risk society, how the readiness to internalise personal responsibility toward risk is not a fact, it is a gratuitous, indemonstrable generalising assumption. Responsibility is more often enforced; but even if a citizen chooses to bear the weight of individual responsibilities by carrying the costs and uncertainties that go with privatised risk, it does not necessarily follow that he will thank neoliberalism's educational therapies. Why should this be viewed as an ungrateful response?

If the above is the reality of governing at a distance, then governing at a distance should not be confused with resurrecting and presumably vindicating the old virtues of *laissez faire* liberalism in its economic and political components. There is nothing that is classically liberal in neoliberalism. The point becomes clearer if we reflect that liberalism has been embedded and practiced within the state, the classical liberal-democratic state. And its practices as government have always been marked, to use trite words, by tolerance, respect, prudence and accommodation; in sum, by a soft use of power toward all its social referents. These practices have gained space because the individual freedoms embodied in liberal thought came to be the indispensable building blocks of political participation and organisation. They were and are freedoms essential for governing together. There is little or nothing, therefore, in past liberal democratic practices of power that anticipates the distancing, marginalising suspicion selectively practiced toward some citizens by neoliberal government. Assisted by a shared narrative, the style of liberal democratic governments has been, to use the term again, the style of social-democracy, or in Polanyi's language, the style of liberal embeddedness. Neoliberalism has greater prospective ambitions. They are not nostalgic, they are not reformist; they are transformative of the individual. In contrast, no democratic government in modern history has ever aimed at placing all aspects of collective and individual life on the autopilot of individual market-like rationality. No government therefore had to apply all of its ingenuity to mold a new, fitting type of man.

To understand the neoliberal pretence to govern lightly at a distance, I sought historical precedents. The example that came immediately to mind was Jeremy Bentham's Panopticon, an ingenious brick and mortar lookout designed to control and govern at a distance, without being seen, without dirtying one's own hands, without vented animosity, yet with soulless determination, the inmates of a number of different total institutions (poorhouses, workhouses, asylums, jails, hospices). Just as in neoliberalism's governing at a distance, the Panopticon assumed that social order and economic progress had been threatened by a defect of individual virtues, perversely fostered among the dispossessed by two centuries of Elizabethan legislation (*see* Ch.2, fn.5). 'Morals reformed – health preserved – industry invigorated – instruction diffused – public burthens [sic] lightened, economy seated, as it were, upon a rock – the Gordian knot of the poor law not cut, but untied [...]', these are the opening words with which Bentham introduced the 1787 pamphlet letter illustrating his project.[5] The pamphlet's pointed finger to the many perverse effects of outdoor relief for the dispossessed is on a par with contemporary neoliberalism's perversity narrative of the Welfare society. Further, neoliberalism's governing at a distance, implemented through New Public Management and the outsourcing of public functions and public-private partnerships, is anticipated in Bentham's proposed delivery of poor relief by means of 250 Panopticon 'Industry Houses', each accommodating 2,000 dependent poor, owned and managed by a national joint-stock company. The narrative in support of the Houses' institutional practices is one of relief, but relief now intended in the active positive sense of re-educating for a productive life.[6] Whatever the narrative, the daily practices are practices of unbending punitive discipline. This explains why Foucault devoted special attention to the idea of the Panopticon as an anticipation of modern society's drive toward the normalisation of discipline in individual and collective life. Bentham's is only one among many intellectual contributions (Malthus, Ricardo, Chadwick, the Poor Law Commissioners' Report of 1834) that preceded and followed the Poor Law Reform Act. Still, as I discuss in the footnote about the Poor Law in Chapter Two, and in the footnote above on Polanyi's treatment of the same issue, the reform represented a relatively short and contained exception in the more linear move of modern liberal states toward forms of social risk solidarity. The New Poor Law preceded, at the first troublesome stirring of the industrial revolution, the successful mobilisation of socially conscious movements; more surprisingly and more daringly, contemporary neoliberalism resurrects with great simpleminded aplomb the New Poor Law's narrative in the context of infinitely more complex economies and societies – as if two hundred years of socially-minded advances and increasing *gouvernementalité* had been two hundred years of blind perversity. But, in the pursuit of a utopian neoliberal programme of guided redemption, anything goes.

Paolo Ceri's cited essay (Ceri 2003) dissects the controlling tools necessary to realise these ambitions of redemption. The essay's telling title is *La società vulnerabile* (*The Vulnerable Society*). In a section of it, he compares two modes of social surveillance. The first one in time is the 'vertical' surveillance offered by the Panopticon, in which the few control the many, and the many are organised in social categories needing different degrees and type of surveillance. The second and more ambitious strengthens the first. It is the 'horizontal' surveillance described in David Lyon's *synopticon* (1994). Here, the many watch and control the one, but the one is also part of the many who watch. Ceri writes,

---

5.   Reprinted by Verso in 1995, Miran Bozovic editor.

6.   Among all of Charles Dickens' novels, *Hard Times* (1854) seems to me to offer the most bleakly sarcastic indictment of Benthamite utilitarianism, not simply for its punitive exploitive features (Oliver Twist's *'Please, sir, I want some more'*) but above all for its dispiriting educational philosophy. In the words of Mr. Gradgrind, founder and headmaster of his model school, (*Hard Times* 'opening words), 'Now, what I want is Facts. Teach these boys and girls nothing but facts. Facts alone are wanted in life. Plant nothing else and root out everything else. You can only form the minds of reasoning animals upon Facts [...] Stick to facts, Sir!'

The new policies are oriented, differently [from the Panopticon], toward the knowledge and manipulation of behavioural and preferential models. It is less a case of keeping order than one of building an order; therefore the purpose is to identify and anticipate [...] The identity of the individual is reconstructed by observing behaviour and preferences in different life spheres, [...] categories are built from the observation of single individuals. (Ceri 2003: 61, my translation)

Antoine Garapon echoes the *synopticon* theme when he writes, 'Neoliberal governmentality activates reciprocal surveillance as a direct product of competition: controlling everybody by controlling oneself and vice versa. Self-control and mutual surveillance become inseparable' (Garapon 2012: 97, my translation).

Given these transformative ambitions, neoliberalism might also remind us of modern despotic regimes, often inclined to moralise, and hence distrust society. However, the comparison ignores a fundamental difference between dictatorship and neoliberalism that goes to the latter's strategic advantage. Dictatorship's moral distrust of society is fed by the fact that, once in power, dictatorships are typically incapable of mobilising and committing society on either their own or society's terms, and regularly denounce this as proof that society is irremediably unable to rise to the moral occasion that dictatorship uniquely offers. So, when it comes to governing, classical dictatorships deal, so to say, in bulk. They work from suspicion and distrust, but they neither can nor care to paper them over. Governing with relaxed, reassuring distance is certainly not part of their propaganda. They do not exhibit the supple persuasive narratives of natural personal regeneration which neoliberalism parades. They work in order to subject. Paramount for them is extracting public conformity; which, easily obtained and dutifully exhibited, is sufficient to impress most of its subjects that dissent is marginal (Kuran 1995). In this sense, dictatorships, especially totalitarian ones, are more driven by their ideology and its ultimate purpose than by subtle and inventive techniques of government. When it comes to techniques, they are at best, more versed in conveniently improvising. Claiming command in the name of ideology is a sufficient guide. Rather, it is people that may develop a panoply of diverse accommodations to reconcile themselves to despotic rule. In contrast to conventional dictatorship, neoliberalism ostensibly claims no commanding ideology. Rather, it publicly declares that it will pursue a reasonable and natural objective: that of divesting its governing self of top-down power and returning decisions to proudly independent individuals. This is the neoliberal narrative, employed to persuade the individual that his stepping-up is possible, decisive, sufficient and beneficial. Individual choices will now prove simple and trustworthy; they will call upon personal responsibility that will be exercised, without a doubt, prudently. What each one of us will need is just a portable abacus. But given that this public narrative proceeds side-by-side with a complex micromanagement of proffered choices, fairly immune in fact to consumer scrutiny, their combination yields *de facto* subjection blurred by the smokescreen of personal autonomy. Undoubtedly, the proffered choices are presented as the opposite of Hobson's – or Henry Ford's – choices (take it or leave it, no choice at all). A Hobson's choice has no ambition to educate; it does not bother with it, it is simply dismissive. Instead, the freedom to choose what neoliberal policies formally offer appears as a freedom to choose between alternative conducts. But is it?

The criminalisation of the other

Neoliberalism has brought about troubling transformations in the criminal justice and adjudication systems. Justice meted out under the law is no longer presented as a matter of plain obedience, equal for all; it is presented as a frame for case-by-case negotiations about utilities. This means that equality of outcomes over similar cases is no longer a necessary criterion under which individual negotiations must be conducted. That said, inequality of outcomes is not randomly distributed. Moreover, not all choices are right for the defendant. The 'right' choices are those that carry degrees of rewards, the 'wrong' ones carry degrees of personal costs. But deciding what is right or wrong is not a simple abacus matter that the justice system graciously leaves to the prudence of the defendant. Rather, defendants' decisions are steered by compulsion and taken under duress. They are usually suboptimal. Not only are individual choices conveniently steered, furthermore, they are inscribed in and further constrained by neoliberalism's securitising priorities. Some analysts therefore find a fundamental ambivalence in the treatment of justice under neoliberalism. As Antoine Garapon (2012) describes it the ambivalence resides in the fact that criminal justice comes to employ both negotiating and securitising strategies. Garapon writes,

> Neoliberalism corresponds *at the same time* to an increase in the liberty of its subjects and to a new way of dominating them […] At the same time as [neoliberalism] homogenizes the penalties […] it develops unprecedented degrees of transaction; at the same time as fixed penalties and drastic laws against recidivism are introduced […] there is a growth in negotiated resolutions. (Garapon 2012: 164, my translation)

The ambivalence, however, is only superficial; securitising is paramount in both strategies. Let me explain by starting with securitising developments in the American criminal justice system. These developments are painstakingly documented and cogently discussed in William Stuntz's extensive excursus (2011, especially Ch.9) on American criminal justice from its inception to today. Mine is only a scant summary of the latest developments, those captured in Stuntz's book title, *The Collapse of American Criminal Justice*. The developments include constant increases in the level of penalties, themselves increasingly graded and fine-tuned; frequent use of life sentences without the possibility of parole; constant subtraction of penalties from judicial discretion; tighter legislation against the threat of recidivism ('three-strikes and you are out' laws are the best case in point); administrative security measures such as curfews for specific demographic groups; residential restrictions not only for released sex offenders (a sex offender is thereby a natural sex predator) but also for other released offenders (denial by law or by administrative act of public housing for some categories of former convicts);

institutional confinement after release from jail to prevent recidivism (in France, *rétention de sûreté*). Foremost among these developments in criminal justice is the increasing power retained by prosecutors. Prosecutorial plea-bargaining is favoured by the increasingly fine-tuned gradation of crime types (there are now, for example, various degrees of sexual assault).[7] It allows prosecutors to criminalise with discretion, by threatening harsher indictments. One result is that almost all criminal cases are adjudicated without a court trial. Further, when criminal cases are mainly in the hands of prosecutors, defence counsel becomes paramount but, even in the rare cases when funds for public defenders are not cut in the name of fiscal responsibility, public defenders for the indigent are not on a par with defenders who are privately hired.[8] All of these prosecutorial tools are aimed at securitising. Such is the case even when the purpose of a criminal provision seems to be quite the opposite. Parole boards are clearly intended to examine evidence justifying pardons or a reduction in the penalty. In practice and for most cases, they have become occasions for censuring the inmate, and reasserting the retributive nature of the penalty. In some cases, parole is denied because the board has reason to believe that the inmate, simply by reason of his demographic profile (race, ethnicity, age) and of previous not necessarily criminal behaviour, would constitute a statistical danger for society. If so, it is not surprising that judges and prosecutors have progressively restricted the revision of *res iudicata* for supervening evidence.[9] No longer does criminal intent exclusively rely on the actual features of a specific crime; it relies in bulk on statistical projections. So much, then, for the certainty of the law. Last among the expressions of the new criminal system is the exponential growth of the prison population. The increase in crime rates has little or nothing to do with it.[10] In the case of the United States, whose prison population more than quadrupled in the last thirty years, the new wave of incarcerations accompanied by aggravation of the penalties involves overwhelmingly minor, victimless crimes committed by others-from-us (street sale and consumption of drugs, including soft ones).[11]

---

7. Increasing differentiation between forms of sexual assault is welcomed, not only by women. But it also increases prosecutorial discretion.

8. Ironically, one of the unanticipated consequences of the transition from the inquisitorial to the accusatorial or adversarial criminal system in the documentary face of a trial (see for example the abolition of the investigating judge, in 1989 in Italy, in 1975 in West Germany) is the increasing importance and cost of appropriate defence counselling.

9. These aspects of domestic criminal justice forge a climate that normalises extra judicial treatment of terrorism as well as the adoption of preventive measures that violate individual rights (the Patriot Act in the USA, Crime and Security Act in the UK). Anti-terrorism legislation may be inspired by a presumed state of exception, but it thrives in a pre-existing securitising culture that has nothing to do with terrorism.

10. *See*, for the long-range analysis of causes and trends, the cited study by Stuntz (especially Chapter 9).

11. *See* Michelle Alexander's well-researched book (2010). The book provides ample evidence dispelling, among many, the myth that the growth in the prison population reflects a growth in criminality. Similar evidence is provided by Stuntz (2011) as well as by official government websites. Alexander's evidence dispels another myth; namely, that the very high and growing level of Afro-American incarcerations for drug sales and consumption reflects proportionally the fact that more Afro-Americans sell and consume drugs. Consumption of cannabis among young Caucasians is actually higher, yet the probability that an Afro-American consumer is detained is five times as high. Similar differences are found between Latin Americans and other Caucasians.

In the analyses by Young (1999) and Garland (2001), the developments above, taken together, reflect a radical change, especially in the United States and the UK, in the policies and practices employed toward criminality. Beginning in the last decades of the past century, the change as described by Garland involves a transition from a Foucauldian 'penal-welfarist' postwar system, ideally intended to return the inmate to society, to a system of penal and police repression, retribution and confinement. One self-defeating yet not unanticipated effect of the new penal system, in particular the increase in the penalties and the growth of the inmate population, is the increase of prison violence, accompanied in a vicious circle by new repressive carcerary practices (indefinite isolation as a discretional, extra-judicial administrative measure), that barbarise inmates and guards alike.[12]

True, as Garapon points out, not all these developments formally remove individual choices in matters judicial; but since they are choices under compulsion, I dare say that they mesh quite nicely with the ultimate task of securitising. There is still freedom – the freedom to accept or reject various levels of lesser self-indictment and punishment, irrespective of actual culpability, in the hope of avoiding worse – but hope is littered all along by the fear-inducing uncertainty that most subjects entertain as to what to expect. *Mens rea* is no longer relevant to those who sit in judgment. These developments are ordinary facets of everyday neoliberal exertions; the facets from the ground up (Foucault's decentralised discipline). The most important fact about these practices is that they nicely serve neoliberal micromanagement of responsible conduct. On one side stands the citizen made mythically responsible and upright by personal choice; on the other stands the criminal, also by choice (obviously his and only his). There are no abstract crimes out there; there are lurking criminals ready to act at any time. But who are they, and when will they strike? Anticipation is of the essence (Ceri's quote above comes to mind). Lawlessness has progressively become a state of affairs that cannot and should not be addressed in the way it is addressed in Mary Douglas' (1992: Ch.1) solidarity society; that is, by separating risk from blame ('no-fault risk'), as well as damage and remedies from *mens rea*. On the contrary, the best response to lawlessness is to make prevention the first step and the first imperative; to reify the danger in the persons of the ever-lurking criminal and the ever-hapless victim. With a little science and a little statistics we can sort out the lurking criminal, classify (what is racial profiling after all?) and, if advisable, confine him. It sounds

---

Police, increasingly relying on predictive methodologies of Situational Crime Prevention, select the neighbourhood to control; detention, often by framing, is discretionary.

12. 'Virtual incarceration' (Holden and Shuler 2013) has been suggested as a way of ameliorating the carcerary system – its overcrowding, violence and costs. It relies on newfangled technologies, mainly electronic monitoring systems, that, taken together, offer the possibility of establishing a sort of benign *synopticon*, limited to the less violent criminals, as 'measured' by predictive risk and geospatial analytics. The low-risk offender is allowed to stay home, under constant surveillance, and with incentives for self-reporting and peer and professional support. There is, however, at least one problem with virtual incarceration. It does not question criminalisation, its escalation and its reasons. A criminal is a criminal because so says the law. Nor for that matter does it question the analytics. On the contrary, it embraces them as all-knowing and revolutionary.

swifter, more effective, and possibly cheaper than programmes of rehabilitation or programmes that attempt to address the causes of crime. So why bother with causes and their treatment, often complex and controversial? Employed for the purpose of efficient prevention, genetics and the sociology of criminal inclinations may best replace justice pursued after the fact.[13] As of late, crucial assistance in the pursuit of prevention can most speedily, hence most admirably, come from Google and Facebook, whose algorithms can profile their users, starting from the users' search patterns. This is no science fiction. This is already beyond the realm of the possible, as documented by Evgeny Morozov (2013).[14] However, this constructed state of pervasive vigilance, in which criminality becomes a constant and surveillance a default on auto-pilot, gives no comfort to the people. On the contrary, it nurtures a popular culture, obsessed beyond the facts[15] by media-fed images of diffuse lawlessness and incumbent disorder, for the control of which even government and its repressive apparatus may, in the end, appear insufficient. Later in the essay, we will see more extensively the many ways in which such pervasive fears feed reciprocal distrust, erode solidarity, and lead some of us, in a genuinely competitive neoliberal spirit, to 'take things in our own hands'.

---

13. In fact, if prevention is first, we could even make it impossible, with an occasional ethical tres-passing, for people to commit crime. In a *New York Times* op-ed of 7 August 2012 (*The Perfect Non-Crime*), Michael L. Rich gives examples. We can develop smart cars that would not go over a given speed, or would stop at a red light no matter what, or would measure the blood-alcohol level of the driver (and perhaps report it to the insurer). There is no right to drive drunk any more than there is a right to drive without a licence. But if a chemical is developed that would suppress the urge to commit crimes, can governments decide to add it to the water supply? Can government control thoughts, or should we be free to think and commit crime and pay after the fact? Are we at risk of losing, by no longer using it, our moral compass? Are we on a slippery slope? If genetics and sociology before the crime can replace justice after the crime, is the sky the limit? What about chemical castration? What about the use of neuroscience to detect criminal inclinations? *See also*, more extensively, Rich (2013).

14. Especially Ch.6 which is aptly titled 'Less Crime, More Punishment'.

15. For example, beginning in the Nineties, there has been, not only in the United States but also in Europe, a fall in the homicide rate. And the reasons have little to do with increasing repression.

Chapter Six

Selling Out State and Law

The pursuit of efficiency

What Garapon described in the previous chapter as ambivalence in neoliberalism's strategies of government could be better described as *escamotage*, a sleight of hand. I have argued time and again that governing at a distance does not mean governing 'without interfering in the social'. On the contrary, it is governing 'without interference by the social', especially the wasteful interference that, in the neoliberal imagination, comes from the reprobate and unreformed, of which there is no scarcity. It is punctilious, bureaucratic governance (I use the neologism on purpose), redeploying new guiding ways and means. These are in fact the ways and means that give credibility to neoliberalism's pretence that it governs at a distance, gently, without really governing. To secure governing at a distance in a way that is natural, efficient and responsible, the preliminary task its advocates invoke is to starve the state's cluttered institutions, immoderate resources, and strangling pretences. Government is the problem, and we can do better and do so more frugally. We need, in the hackneyed saying, more market and less state. Taxation deprives people of the wealth they alone create (narrowing tax rate differentials or outright regressive taxation might be a solution; those who produced more wealth should only gently be squeezed).[1] Taxation should be replaced by fees covering only those services the citizen as consumer requires; also, we should pay for demonstrated output, not for input). For all these purposes we ultimately need an 'ownership society', which keeps and manages what it produces. A society so endowed is in a better position to make government accountable, to secure first of all that governments live within their means. Further, the lesser those means are, the better. This may help explain why neoliberalism is opportunistic when it comes

---

1.   Lower tax rates on capital gains are just one example; another is across the board exemption of real estate mortgage interests. In both cases, wealthier people are advantaged, hence they are induced to invest - be it financially, at home or abroad, or in Hollywood mansions. But the most famous and most furiously contested example of regressive taxation is the flat-rate poll- tax (formally Community Tax) introduced in 1988 by Margaret Thatcher's Conservative government. It was regressive in that it charged each unit a fixed amount time the number of adult residents (hence poll tax), irrespective of the unit's property value. However, Thatcher's poll tax was not so much meant to regressively redistribute income. More ambitiously, it was meant to curb expenditures by local government by also placing local government, with the help of other legislative measures, under tighter central control. The actual consequences on poorer rate payers and poorer communities, plus its inefficiencies and rigidities (Self 1993: 189–92), were such that the tax was quickly amended by John Major, when he replaced Thatcher as Conservative prime minister.

to fiscal responsibility. The moral goal is not to balance the budget so that the state prudently lives within its means, but to deprive the artificial state of its unduly appropriated and improperly used means, no matter what it takes: by denying the state fiscal resources; by pushing it to the welcome brink of insolvency; by starving it.

To obtain this, we reinvent government. One default point is the adoption of the principles of 'New Public Management'. NPM involves the introduction of painstaking management principles on the quantitative cost-benefit analysis of the services the consumer requests. In a way, there is nothing particularly new about the general idea of rational management. The utopia of scientific management has a long and honourable tradition of its own; and quantification is presumably the utmost of formal rationality. It shall take us from messy, obscure and aimless politics to apparently neat, transparent and consequential administration. This old administrative utopia may explain why NPM has made inroads not only in the United States and other Anglo-Saxon democracies but in rational France and by-the-book Germany, as well as in developing nations (conditionalities attached to loans and debt relief by international organisations).

Assuming for a moment that government's central role is to provide consumer services, we might feel that there is nothing wrong with aiming at effectiveness, efficiency and transparency in what the state delivers. They sound at first as respectable and desirable objectives. They also seem quantifiable objectives, the fulfilment of which is easy to operationalise and verify. If the state acts effectively and if its actions are transparent, the citizen can take stock of his/her own gains and of the government's costs. But efficiency is not always that simple to define and pursue, and whether simple or not, it may interfere with other desirable goals.

Here is a major case of efficiency simply defined and pursued but undesirable in its effects. Speaking of New Public Management as applied to French justice, Garapon writes,

> Efficiency redefines judicial activity, which becomes a *product* [...] [with] a perverse effect, that of correlating any evaluation of justice with what is measurable, that is [,] to time and money [...], all to the disadvantage of what is not measurable, [...] which is disqualified as non measurable and therefore secondary. (Garapon 2012: 39, my translation)

Later on, Garapon concludes, 'Instead of considering the new public management a simple technocratic discourse (replacing others), we must consider it as a redefinition of the [justice] institution' (Garapon 2012: 52). When measurement and efficiency rise, as in Garapon's example, to the status of intrinsic values, nothing more needs to be said about the beneficial performance of the system; the former absorbs the latter. Efficiency slides from being a means into being a goal, a pure and simple case of goal displacement. The expected output is no longer the efficiency of chosen outputs; rather, efficiency chooses its convenient outputs.

There are, in addition, many policy domains within which the ostensible pursuit of efficiency is far from easy. But since, as in Garapon's example, neoliberal emphasis on output efficiency is not motivated by academic obsession with correct methodological measurement but by a narrowly construed understanding of public service, neoliberal governments may still squeeze through with a mere semblance of efficiency. When determination is not in the hands of a single agent, as it happens under neoliberalism's public-private schemes of government, each agent uses partially different notions of efficiency. In addition, some of the criteria are less than objective, as they tend to mix a desire for easy quantification with preconceptions and expectations that give quantification a biased turn. Hence, any effort to reach agreement turns out to be fraught with difficulties. The response to this state of affairs has been the creation of a self-multiplying but also self-devouring jungle of overlapping norms, codes, standards, techniques, procedures, audits, certifications fancifully described by some scholars as post-bureaucratic and (why not), post-Weberian. It is a jungle of destructive creation more than creative destruction. Béatrice Hibou gives a relentless account of these phenomena in a book aptly titled *La bureaucratisation du monde à l'ère néolibérale* (Hibou 2012: Ch.3). Previously, I provisionally labelled the phenomena as unanticipated consequences of governing at a distance. However, they are more than that.

Neoliberalism asserts that its pursuit of efficiency is simply what consumers want, and that consumers know what they mean when they speak of efficiency. But when it comes to consumers, the assertion is, consciously or unconsciously, false on both counts. It is also a mystification when it implies that neoliberal governments just do what consumers want: by not interfering they presumably let consumers pursue what they already want. Consumer demands are not demands of and by consumers any more than public opinion (its demands, preferences and expectations) is opinion *of* and *by* the public. Just as public opinion in general is more often than not opinion found *in* the public, so consumer demands in particular are more often than not demands created by what the market,[2] in our case, government as market, offers.[3] And just as private economic markets come

---

2. One case in point: when black pearls first appeared on the market, nobody wanted them. When they were shown together with other jewellery and priced high the sellers biased the price by exploiting what psychologists and behavioural economists came to call 'anchoring heuristics'.

3. Walter Lippmann's healthy scepticism, expressed in both *The Phantom Public* and *Public Opinion*, about public opinion as autonomously formed, fixed and all-knowing is today just as valid as it was almost a century ago. In fact, owing to the information revolution of the last decades, his scepticism is in some ways even more valid today. Lippmann writes, 'Man[…] is the creature of an evolution who can just about span a sufficient portion of reality to manage his survival, and snatch what on the scale of time are but a few moments. Yet this same creature has invented ways of seeing what no naked eye could see, of hearing what no era could hear, of weighing immense masses and infinitesmal (sic) ones […] Gradually he makes for himself a trustworthy picture inside his head of the world beyond his reach' (Lippman 1922: 29). But those evolved ways of seeing, of hearing, of weighing do not lift Lippmann's scepticism. For one thing, that personal picture is not trustworthy, as there cannot exist 'in the hearts of men a knowledge of the world beyond their reach' (Lippman 1922:31). We replace it with shortcuts that are rarely, if such a quality is conceivable, foolproof. What we accept as knowledge proceeds from informational

in many shapes, all characterised by degrees of organisational and promotional control on which consumers have little to say, so also governments are decisive in determining what goods and services they offer and how. They may for instance choose to provide collective services (defined benefit retirement), or more individualised, fragmented services (defined contribution retirement). So choices must be made and are made, by neoliberal policy-makers no less. Whatever their domain, there is nothing automatic about the decisional processes that lead to them. And here lies the mystification. A government that has decided to pare down its performance to a string of automatic efficiency accountings, presumably placing government on autopilot, has nonetheless exercised, like all governments, a choice in a context of other available policies and practices. The government must have weighed its choices against others. Whatever the domain of policy actions, the choices must also be assessed for their collective and prospective impacts, their repercussions, their spillover and demonstration effects. These are best understood as outcomes rather than outputs, and outcomes are not easy to quantify, especially in monetary terms. Outcomes also have the disadvantage of being affected by unintended consequences and external events that are difficult to forecast. But this is the appropriately challenging nature of democratic decision-making. Furthermore, choices must often deal with the difficult allocation of limited budgetary resources; that is, with costs and benefits in the perspective of distributive justice. For example, a defendant is entitled to a public defender. But the entitlement can never be absolute. It becomes actionable if and only if sufficient money is allocated to it. What makes money sufficient depends on allocation decisions that go beyond budgetary constraints. Budgetary constraints are a constant. Hence, justice requires eminently political distributive decisions.[4] These are the kinds of decisions that, incidentally, allow opposition politicians to boycott the implementation of a law or the performance of a public office by cutting their budgets. In sum, giving priority to efficiency is itself a political choice, but once made, it aims at removing the need for more open and complex democratic deliberations.

---

sources that are limited and that further, for subjective and objective reasons, we are not in the position to fully verify. And even if, naïvely, we were to take for good that those informational sources are nowadays becoming not only unlimited, but also open and transparent, as the Internet revolution promises, the journey from full information to full knowledge, assuming that we are desirous of embarking on it, is long and poorly-mapped, the more so in fact the more information we are regaled with. In Chapter Seven, I will say more on the solutionist pretences of the Internet, and their affinity with the pretences of neoliberalism. In the text above, I resume the discussion of efficiency as a presumptive public want.

4. Distributive decisions are not available to a judge. Since a judge makes single decisions seriatim, s/he has no benchmark by which to compare and allocate. It follows that once a judge decides that an entitlement, the respect of which requires money, is legally absolute and allocates accordingly, other entitlements later judged as similarly absolute may nevertheless come up short. We are left with a sort of oxymoron: the selectivity of absolute entitlements. It reminds me of the oxymoronic command contained in Art. 112 of the Italian Constitution: 'the public prosecutor has the obligation to institute criminal proceedings'.

Selling state and law

Ezra Suleiman offers a relevant comment on the issue of efficiency, which takes us to a related facet of neoliberal practices. Suleiman writes,

> for some politicians [...] the reinvention of government is a call for [...] more efficient [government] [...] For others [...] it is essentially a political program *whose* aim is to curtail the activities and duties of the government, to curtail its obligations to society, and, most important, to curtail the obligations of citizens to their own society. (Suleiman 2003: 52)[5]

The statement may be correct in principle. But when efficiency is part of the neoliberal agenda, the demarcation between the two objectives and between those who advocate one or the other becomes empty. The pursuit of efficiency and accountability merges with the pursuit of lean government, of down-sizing and right-sizing.[6] Altogether, these objectives serve the same purpose. Contracting private firms for the purpose of running public services serves to insert the logic of the market in government operations. Contracting out or outsourcing takes various forms and is done in various degrees, depending on which services, tasks and resources are delegated, and with what degree of autonomy. However, they all come with prices attached. I argued in my closing remarks about the New Public Management that the search for efficiency and its measurement comes at the price of displacing the broader distributive goals of democratic government. Some of the same can be argued in the case of private-public partnerships and outsourcing. Minimally, such partnerships come at the price of democratic accountability. Both horizontal accountability, exercised between and within public institutions, and vertical accountability, exercised by citizens on public institutions, are difficult to secure when they are applied to exclusively public institutions. But the difficulties deepen and multiply when, believing that the problems reside in the fact that the institutions called to give account are public, we try and replace public logic with market logic. When public institutions delegate, delegation goes easily beyond administrative and executive tasks. Whether explicitly meant to do so or not, delegating leads to the transfer of decisional powers.

Delegating raises constitutional and deontological questions about Weberian state sovereignty when to be delegated are functions that touch on the state's monopoly of force, such as defence, the armed forces and armaments, justice,

---

5. Suleiman offers an extensive and richly documented comparative analysis of the various aspects pertaining to the reinvention of government. The result is a complex picture of the phenomenon. In it, the United States emerges as the most extreme adopter (more so than Europe and Japan) of socioeconomic policies with a neoliberal imprint.

6. The removal of redundancy as costly and non-competitive is another objective. In institutional analysis, the concept of redundancy once had a positive cybernetic connotation. This was especially so in the case of American public institutions, given federalism, separation of powers, checks and balances. Martin Landau writes, 'there are good grounds for suggesting that efforts to improve public administration by eliminating duplication and overlap would, if successful, produce just the opposite effect' (Landau 1969: 349).

prisons, police forces, security.[7] I will not treat those questions. I will limit myself to an incidental reflection pertaining to the neoliberal administration of law and order. I anticipated the essence of the reflection in the closing paragraph of the previous chapter. There I suggested that, instead of assuaging popular fears, the development of a newly repressive criminal system increases popular obsession with diffuse daily lawlessness and motivates people to 'take matters in their own hands'. Here, I suggest another cause of that motivation. Citizens' inclination to take up personal protection from lawlessness and from social risks is also fostered, in a sort of cultural contagion, by neoliberal governments' inclination to privatise essential state tasks.[8] On the side of government, we witness the replacement of compulsory military service with professional armies; the outsourcing of various defence functions, including the use of force, to private mercenary contractors; the private management of prisons; and the parting of criminal justice from the law-given certainty of punishment in favour of a growing emphasis on the rights of the actual and prospective victims (stand your ground self-defence laws). On the side of citizens, we witness the hiring of private police; the purchase of arsenals of guns for claimed self-protection; the growth of gated communities; the formation of neighbourhood watches and patrols; and calls for personalised criminal justice administered in the name of the victims, their relatives and neighbours. As to criminal justice, the growing emphasis that legislation, prosecutors and (if a criminal case goes that far) judges place on the plight of the victims implies a view of criminal justice as previously indifferent to the victims and over indulgent toward the criminals. The victim becomes the archetype of a defenceless society, perpetually exposed to naturally inclined predators. Plight becomes hands-on right, a human right for utilitarian purposes (Garapon 2012: 67). The victim acquires a fictional authority as representative of other prospective victims. Still, let it be clear, he is not *the* representative of other victims; rather, his case represents one of many similar cases. There is no solidarity; there is fearful individualism.[9] By this logic, where the impersonality of the law is replaced by a sort of case-by-case

---

7.   In the case of national defence, the pursuit of lean government is not the main reason for out-sourcing (Wulf 2007). Nonetheless, the issue remains, especially when outsourcing takes unusual dimensions.

8.   This cultural contamination is acutely examined by Joerg Friedrichs (2010). His article offers a systematic analysis of various gradients of privatisation and distinguishes and exemplifies side-by-side two recipients of state outsourcing: the market (New Public Management, outsourcing of state force and, finally, commodification); and the people (from the state's monopoly of force to certified autonomy, managed segmentation and, finally, community self-help).

9.   Worth noticing is the fact that no American law requires that a person assist others who have been injured or are otherwise in peril, unless the person is implicated in the occurrence. At the same time, Good Samaritans who inadvertently cause further damage may be sued. In 2012, San Francisco policemen did not run to the rescue of a person drowning in the ocean, right in front of their eyes, because they had not been trained for rescue operations. In March 2013, a nurse working in a Californian independent living facility refused, despite emergency-dispatcher prodding, to perform cardiopulmonary resuscitation on a resident because the policies of the company running the facility expressly disallowed such assistance by its personnel.

contractualism (Garapon 2012), why not give the victim the right to assist the prosecutor or occasionally the judge in drafting the sentence?

I return now to the general treatment of public-private partnerships and outsourcing, irrespective of the government functions they cover. Like New Public Management, partnership and outsourcing promise efficiency, transparency, accountability - three different criteria that are not always equally achievable. Practically all the critical considerations I offered in regard to these criteria and to their pursuit when dealing with NPM apply here too. In addition, public-private cooperation presents special problems of coordination, management and supervision, leading, as documented by Hibou (2012), to even more bureaucratisation than in the NPM case. In view of the fact that outsourcing of the same functions may be multiple (including outsourcing the control of outsourcing) as well as chain-like, with subcontractors contracting out in turn, the involved firms and agencies may come to constitute a complex network, hierarchically but also horizontally connected. It then becomes difficult to define and attribute responsibilities in the chains of connectivities, to keep records of the assigned responsibilities, and to verify that actions are in keeping with responsibilities. It is also difficult to define how many of the actors involved are entitled to seek account and, if so, from which link in the chain of responsibilities. Seeking account is not the same as obtaining it, and obtaining it in its correct form, even if the agency called to account intends to report responsibly. If and when obtained, correct evaluation is not automatic. There are many reasons why all these administrative steps are fraught with uncertainty in their conduct and results. The first, overarching reason, I suggest, is the fact that, while bureaucratised, partnerships cannot count on one factor that, though insufficient, makes it possible for a public bureaucracy to operate in an accountable fashion. I am referring to the formal impersonal rationality of conduct that only a public bureaucracy, being public, is in the position to offer. There is nothing impersonal in the contractualism that marks bureaucratised partnerships.

Under certain conditions, a public bureaucracy is still conceivable whose performance is verifiably guided by knowledge, committed resources and what Giorgio Freddi (1989) calls, receptivity.[10] The behaviour of a public bureaucracy is in principle subject to public and internal accountability (*see* discussion of *parrhesia*); expectations about performance are not excised when violated (they are 'more honour'd in the breach than the observance' (Hamlet)). Bureaucratic conduct is to be defined by legal codes and not by flexible contract. It is further defined by the identity codes internal to public institutions and their members. These necessary conditions are not easily available when public functions are contracted out. Contracting out does not alter the private for-profit motives of those who enter into a contract. Also, many contractors are quite large, not by accident but because they are more likely, given their technical resources and their

---

10. Speaking of knowledge and expertise, Freddi argues that these can well be patrimony of a reformed bureaucracy, in which knowledge prevails on legal hierarchies.

abundant political connections, to obtain contracts. A new kind of business for profit has been born. Once contractors are in business and the partnership has become operative, the larger the contractors, the greater their ability to influence public bureaucracies and governments. This helps explain why outsourcing may escape dutiful verification. When controls arrive, they usually arrive late, either because they are not prioritised or because of understaffing. Moreover, they are triggered by mass media scoops, lead to political and parliamentary investigations, and raise not only the issue of management but also that of political responsibility, with its possible legal and criminal implications.[11]

---

11. In the United States the use of outsourcing is quite common and the caseload that accompanies it is substantial. On the outsourcing of functions related to military defence, *see* Verkuil (2007), especially Chapter 7 on constitutional implications.

Chapter Seven

Old and New Risks: Neoliberalism's Precautionary Opportunism

Premise

So far, my attention has been on social risks. Their long-standing collective remedies have been dismissed, in fact deconstructed and flipped over, by neoliberal policies. Dismissal has coincided with transformations in the so-called work society that are increasing those risks and diversifying their sources. Thus, in what Ulrich Beck (2000) famously calls the new risk society, neoliberalism trivialises a major risk of early and late modernity as a matter of irresponsible individual conduct. The level of analysis has been changed. There is no risk society; there are no systemic social risks that cannot be corrected by ready and willing individuals. Beck's risk society happens to be the society where neoliberalism operates.

But there is much more about Beck's risk society. In addition to social risks, other risks lie in wait. I am referring, to begin with, to the various manifestations of ecological risk. To be sure, ecological risks are not new, nor is it new that the ecological risks may be caused by us. One easy example of ecological risks, in fact of ecological disasters at the hand of humankind is also a very old one. I am referring to widespread deforestation, a common occurrence wherever vast forests thrived. The consequences: soil erosion, landslides, silting, floods, even climate change. Other calamities that some of us may still consider natural, like earthquakes, may also be directly caused by human activity, or their effects may be accentuated by human negligence. One contemporary example is related to the new mega-dam on the Minjiang River, China. According to some seismologists, the 2008 Sichuan earthquake might have been less intense, or would have been delayed, had it not been for the construction of the dam. As to the human contribution to earthquake damage, this depends not only on earthquake magnitude but also, and perhaps more so, on where, in earthquake-prone areas, we build as well as how much we build and in what way. For the rest, an earthquake is impartial.[1] What is new, however, with regard to natural and ecological risks is the escalation and greater severity of their manifestations. This is one reason why we tend to be more aware of them. New awareness is also fed by the exponential growth of scientific and technological know-how which is a source of trust but also a source of warnings

---

1. Not all human manipulations of nature are negative, for nature and for humanity. Genetic manipulations both ancient and modern are responsible for the bounty diversity and quality of the foods nature provides us with. Michael Pollan (2002) offers an engaging historical and anthropological essay on the contribution of horticultural know-how to human nutrition and tastes.

about inappropriate or misplaced uses and a source of material as well as value concerns. In some areas the advance of know-how stems from an unprecedented increase in science's capacity to manipulate nature. However, this is a capacity that is not without its own risks of unknown size, frequency and probability.

New risks, plus new awareness, plus enduring social risks, plus the new insecurities the latter carry because of troubling but politically disregarded social transformations, all give credit to the designation of contemporary society as risk society. Today as at no other time, risks and costs are engaging and mobilising public concern. However, awareness and mobilisation are also remarkably selective.

On the measurement of risk

A new research literature has burgeoned, dedicated to the complexities of risks – new risks especially – as well as risk assessments and human responses to them. Before moving to the attitude of neoliberalism in regard to new risks, the literature deserves our attention. Some of the new risk categories are potentially catastrophic but probability, timing and level, as well as the relative performance of alternative measures, are often hard to assess. Therefore, risks are hard to control. In some cases timing is at issue not in the sense of whether but, rather, of when (i.e. the melting of the polar icecap). In other cases uncertainty has to do with the probability of the risky event – not when but whether it will occur. In yet others we may know that the effects of a risk will be immediate, but we do not know how serious and widespread they will be. Toxic emissions from a factory usually have an immediate impact on the neighbourhood, but because of other factors beyond human control (rain, winds, orography, etc.) we may not know how dangerous the emissions will prove to be, how far they will travel or how fast they will disperse. Uncertainty and its accompanying fears may feed or be fed by a distrust of institutional expertise. Institutional expertise changes rapidly; experts clash; some new risks are manufactured by technological advances intended to improve knowledge, including hands-on knowledge of risks. Today's deeper awareness of risk is not so much the result of a larger number of risks but the result of a growing awareness that we (some of us) share responsibility for them – in manufacturing them, in addressing them inappropriately, or in running away from them. In addition, as I anticipated in a previous chapter, for some categories of old risks (aging, sickness, disabilities) alertness to risk is less the result of increasing fears than of immoderately increasing expectations – that sickness, aging, death itself have reason to be no more; hence their acceptance is somehow even immoral. For all categories of risk we may say that risk is less and less a given state of affairs. Measuring, assessing and addressing risks cannot be separated from the subjectivities – in the public and among decision-makers – that nourish them.

As to the public, many risks, especially today, exercise an easily spreading morbid, even alluring concern; one that may prove excessive when compared to other risks, old and new, and to facts on the ground. For example, the public attention that a major calamity, bloody and unexpected, elicits may instate a vicious circle. Instantly spread by the media, collective fears feed the media, which keeps feeding the alarm. So sustained, the emotional resonance of the event may lead to perceiving the event as more probable than it actually was and remains. This is the essence of what is known as the availability bias: people make judgments about the probability of events by the ease and vividness with which examples come to mind.[2] Niklas Luhmann writes, 'Risk awareness today shows [...] a fascination with the probability of extremely improbable occurrences, which – when they do happen – constitute a disaster. This cannot be explained alone by the fact that technology offers such possibility' (Luhman 1993: ix). Still, this does not mean that the presence of a serious and probable risk will invariably feed apprehension. Risks that are serious and probable but somehow fail to obtain emotional resonance may elicit little attention. If a risk is constantly present and active, in fact if it is no longer a risk but a reality, it may feed habituation and fade into the background. If a risk exhibits constant cumulative but trickling effects, the effects may go unnoticed. These uncertainties, objective and subjective, as to levels and probabilities of risk leave decision makers with no clear instructions. Experts and decision makers who seriously intend to find responses to risk that are technically correct and shared by the public may experience frustration.[3] More 'adventurous'

---

2. Memory plays a role, certainly in my case. In the sixties two environmental scares reached dimensions that mobilised government action, in one case at the international level. The first scare followed the discovery of near-global radioactive fallout due to atmospheric nuclear weapons tests conducted by the USA and Russia after the end of the war. The second scare, following the discovery of widespread pesticide poisoning, reached its acme with the publication of Rachel Carson's *Silent Spring*. However, how many people now remember the climate of fear created by these two discoveries? I report it here because I just happened to run into a review article of a book on the life of Rachel Carson.

3. Sometimes, public measures may cause odd, perhaps unwanted, reactions in the public. For example, public opinion being somehow scared by an imagined danger, authorities may decide to alleviate the scare by faking decisively radical measures against what does not exist. The result is to confirm in the public that the danger was real. One case is narrated by Alessandro Manzoni in the *I promessi sposi* ([1825] 1909: 534-5). It was a commonly held belief that the Milano plague, during which the novel takes place, was spread on purpose by *untori* (anointers). In one case, Manzoni reports, 'Some persons who fancied they had seen people, [...] in the cathedral, anointing a partition [...], had this partition, and a number of benches enclosed within it, brought out during the night; although the President of the Board of Health, [...] having inspected the screen, the benches, and the stoups of holy water, and found nothing that could confirm the ignorant suspicion of a poisonous attempt, had declared, to humour other people's fancies, and *rather to exceed in caution, than from any conviction of necessity* that it would be sufficient to have the partition washed. This mass of piled-up furniture produced a strong impression of consternation among the multitude, to whom any object so readily became an argument. It was said, and generally believed, that all the benches, walls, and even the bell-ropes in the cathedral, had been rubbed over with unctuous matter.' On the other hand, there were also dismissive characters like Manzoni's don Ferrante who on his death bed kept asserting, on the strength of syllogistic reasoning buttressed by his astrological studies, the only ones available to him, the utter impossibility of contagion. The stars, he claimed, did me in. No cognitive dissonance for him. A bizarre scenario; but no less bizarre than the opposite scenario; one involving what may be called voluntary risks. In it, the authorities embark on a public campaign to impress upon consumers the real and serious personal danger represented by some of their recurring voluntary behaviours (speeding, smoking, poor eating habits, drinking) or omissions (not wearing a seat belt). The use of extremely gory

decision makers may instead feel freer to act and find remedies to these uncertainties; in fact they may lift uncertainty by appealing to their own capacity for persuasion. Uncertainties may, in the last analysis, be removed by asserting a superior need which admits no hesitations. This is facilitated if public opinion does not coalesce on risks and remedies (as it coalesced in the past century around social risks). Such is the arena within which neoliberal policies in regard to risk may, as from the title of this chapter, opportunistically operate. Let us even assume what is extremely unlikely: that a series of features of a risk – nature, probability, timing, level and spread of the damages – are firm and uncontroversial. Still, this is rarely sufficient to point out for sure what measures should be taken, in what order of priority, within what cost parameters, by whom or in assistance to whom. Even in the case of extreme dangers, facts do not speak as facts and cannot at any rate decide for us. At first, Beck is terse and firm, saying: 'The prospect of catastrophes represents a barrier to calculation. We want to avoid it at all costs – even if it is extremely improbable'. But in the same page he steps back, and rightly so:

> But what is the catastrophe threshold beyond which quantitative calculations are no longer convincing? [...] The really interesting question is what counts as a catastrophe. And that is presumably a question which will be answered very differently by decision-makers and victims. (Beck 2008, p. 118)

In addition, the question may well be answered very differently among decision-makers and victims alike. This means that agreement on what constitutes a catastrophe is rare, not just because real catastrophes are rare and we should not panic but because the distinction is one of degrees, and degrees (in most cases) are also subjective. Among experts and decision makers, relevant disagreement goes beyond objective technical assessments. It involves values, beliefs and interests that may internally divide both experts and decision makers. Further, values, beliefs and interests do not pertain only to the risk at issue, they also and most likely concern other risk areas that the risk at issue may impact upon. For all these reasons, catastrophes, as well as risks in general, most often reside in the eye of the beholder. If the beholders intend to be in charge, their subjectivities make a difference.

One example of interaction between two areas of risk is that between economic growth and the protection of natural resources. Some allege that the former may suffer at the hand of the latter. The conflicts and disagreements are deep-lying; they show imperviousness to evidence, when this is available. As long as we assign absolute preeminence to one of the two areas, as long as (for instance) nature is placed at the service of economic development, as it has been and often continues to be under the impetus of industrial development, the clash between the two spheres

---

images and disturbing narratives may produce the opposite reaction: it does not happen to me, I am a much better driver than the average person (everybody actually believes so); also, the campaign exaggerates consequences so as to get attention. In essence, an optimism bias operates here as a default position.

will continue to be fed by zero-sum visions of the respective solutions. Zero-sum visions are such because what may tilt policy formulations are not objective levels of uncertainties as to the nature of the respective risks, nor the dispassionate calculus of costs and benefits, but values, ideologies, preconceptions, narratives and 'animal spirits'. They all contribute to a sort of hybridisation or contamination of knowledge. As the title of their 1992 book tells us, Douglas and Wildavsky's *Risk and Culture: An essay on the selection of technological and environmental dangers* is precisely about such contaminations.

The *ad hoc* uses of the precautionary principle

Contamination is active even when a variety of factors, either objective or presumed so, announce a catastrophe. Catastrophes would typically suggest a drastic recourse to the so-called precautionary principle in order to avoid or tame them. Instinctively, the principle appears to make sense. In truth, however, the principle in and of itself gives no definitive instructions. Once in the hands of decision makers, it lends itself to *ad hoc* employment from case to case and within the same type of case. One big factor in its variable use is knowledge contamination. I intend this as a factual statement, not as a value judgment (not yet). I am not condemning variable use per se. I am not denouncing the selected, flexible appeal to the precautionary principle; I am illustrating it. To illustrate selected use, I will discuss two concrete examples. In the first example, recourse to the principle is invoked; in the second its use is dismissed. Neither, to put it conservatively, is immune to contamination effects. A premise: there are different versions of drastic action in response to the precautionary principle, and we will see later that the difference is important. In one drastic version, the principle explicitly prescribes an overdose of caution. Beck's version, cited above, was (at first) the most drastic: if the prospect of a catastrophe is at play, then we must act promptly, without regard for costs and probabilities. So much for the prescription, but assuming knowledge, is knowledge actually sufficient to lead to action? Beck hesitates, asking what counts as a real catastrophe. One possibility is that the label 'catastrophe' is used for self-serving purposes. Here, is the first concrete example. The most drastic implementation of the principle was invoked in November 2001 by Richard Cheney, then America's vice-president. But the invocation of the principle was consciously self-serving. It found fame as the 1 per cent doctrine. Speaking about Pakistan's nuclear program, Cheney apparently commented (the exact quote from various Internet sources is uncertain), 'If there's a 1 per cent chance that Pakistani scientists are helping al-Qaeda build or develop a nuclear weapon, we have to treat it as a certainty in terms of our response'.[4] Here, a rhetorical statement saves the

---

4. This reasoning brings to mind a sentence by a local Italian judge who, in October 2012, condemned government seismologists who failed to alert the population of the city of L'Aquila on the presumed probability of an imminent earthquake following a series of minor tremblors. There followed an earthquake that proved disastrous. But seismologists are not in the position to predict a major earthquake, let alone its imminence. The occurrence of minor seismic manifestations,

rhetorician from the annoyance of submitting evidence. In the summer of 2002, the same person proposed a national programme of smallpox vaccination in view of a possible bacteriological attack by Saddam Hussein's regime. Vaccination was bravely invoked despite the fact that it would have killed a few hundred people and infected thousands. The same 1 per cent doctrine was invoked by the second President Bush as one of the recurring justifications for the invasion of Iraq. Incidentally, this example and the previous ones show how the answer to a risk, real, suspected or fabricated, may bring about its own risks. Therefore, responses to a risk should also try and calculate other risks, whether already present or potentially triggered by those responses.

Examples instead of neglect of the precautionary principle come from some of the responses to the new ecological risks (other responses may, in contrast, be of the drastic type). Some current ecological predicaments would seem to lend themselves to drastic applications of the precautionary principle. We could in fact appeal to two version of it, one the mirror image of the other. In its first version, if unanimous scientific evidence does not yet exist ruling out the ecological danger of a proposed human intervention on nature (such as with an open-sky mine), it is the duty of the proposing party to provide the evidence. No evidence of danger is not evidence of no danger. Second version: the high probability of serious risks for health and the environment demands regulations and policies that address them, even if evidence is not final and projected costs are high. In practice, however, we know that when it comes, for instance, to environmental policies, in the United States and elsewhere the two mirror-image versions of the principle have received mixed attention. Preference has more often than not gone to weaker versions of the same. Weak versions may reach a point where precaution slips into proneness to risk. For example, we may approve use-technologies because there is insufficient evidence of a danger to the environment. But if that evidence is indeed insufficient, in so doing we invert the burden of proof. Lack of hard evidence is taken as sufficient proof that risk is limited or absent [5]

---

even in an area at risk, is unrelated to major quakes. The verdict is an invitation to seismologists to protect themselves by predicting an earthquake any time a chair squeaks, which is equivalent to remaining silent.

5. To offer an example from a different policy area, this is the principle applied by the US Supreme Court in denying the last-minute appeal of a death-row inmate. The appeal was based on the risk, advanced by some experts, that the last injection, the lethal one, may cause excruciating pain, but the paralysis produced by previous injections may hide any manifestation of pain. Lack of evidence in support of the defence's argument was the motivation rejecting the appeal. Obviously, there is also no evidence that the procedure causes no pain. Another weak version of the precautionary principle is to make assumptions based on the institutional expertise in matters of risk that decision makers presumably possess. In a recent case, a federal appellate court rejected the appeal of an environmental organisation against the Army Corps of Engineers' mineral exploitation licences in the state of Virginia. As summarised in the *New York Times* of 14 February 2009, the federal court rejected the appeal by declaring that the Corps had the expertise to issue such licences. Expertise may be a necessary opening criterion, especially if risk is notoriously manufactured, but it cannot be taken for granted.

The difference just introduced in the examples above, between drastic appeals to the precautionary principle in some cases and laxity in others, does not seem to be justified and should not at any rate be sought only in factual differences in the respective level of seriousness and probability of risk. In matters of risk, facts as facts are not always beyond dispute. For example, even assuming that the Iraqi regime represented a probable risk for American security, its asserted imminence was far from indisputable. But imminence was invoked; imminence was part of the narrative for public consumption. Many ecological risks, on the other hand, are, so to say, already beyond imminence. They are no longer risks, they are an unfolding reality. Their effects have been, are and will in the future be with us. They are continuous, cumulative and in some cases irreversible. Yet they are often contested, even rejected out of hand. Why the difference? One facilitating factor: the effects build up gradually, the build-up is usually not noticeable from one moment to the next. But beyond this, the difference reflects a subjectively construed justification of the precautionary principle.

The examples I have used were meant to explain why the precautionary principle lends itself to either subjective application or to subjective dismissal, depending on the case.[6] Can we do better by recourse to the 'maximin' principle? According to the principle, if we know that all well-intentioned policies nonetheless carry bad consequences, we choose policies that promise the least worst outcome. The principle sounds like simplicity itself. But it is not. The invasion of Iraq makes the point in more than one way. Let us charitably assume that the invasion honestly appeared to be the least worst policy (the maximin principle assumes honesty). Still, the effects of the invasion proved disastrous in many ways (to the 'surprise' of some supporters of the invasion). Was invasion still the least worst option? And if so, compared to what? The maximin principle requires a level of precision in comparing results often unfolding over time that is impossible to secure in most real situations. Certainly, the invasion proved to be a disaster, but let us charitably assume that the disaster came as an honest surprise, and it came, as it were, after the facts. Therefore, shouldn't the United States have invaded, if it had reliable evidence that an imminent attack was probable? Even in this hypothetical case, where I present the American administration as basically well-meaning and relatively well-informed, there is no easy maximin answer. The nature and size of Saddam Hussein's threatened attack, the capacity of the American military to prevent it, rebut it, deflect it, and minimise it, are all debatable issues that the maximin principle could not cover. By the same token, even a hypothetically better outcome of the invasion – better as in least worst – preceded by a fairly honest assessment of Saddam Hussein's real threats would

---

6. Cass Sunstein (2005) offers a systematic treatment of the principle and its failure to give us unique guidance. Normative judgments are themselves a factor in the failure. Sunstein writes, 'Why don't the very [...] [cautionary] arguments that support the war in Iraq or aggressive regulation of genetic modification of food, also argue against the war in Iraq, or against aggressive regulation of genetic modification of food? Mightn't neglect of the long term, and excessive optimism, be responsible for that very war and that very regulation?' (Sunstein 2005: 41).

have given us only suboptimal guidance. This is not a counsel for inaction. It is a prudent statement in regard to the assistance that precautionary principles can provide us with.

To return to the subjective use of the precautionary principle, a perfect example is offered by the controversies surrounding the peaceful use of nuclear energy. The risks associated with the operation of a nuclear plant are very low as to probability, but horrendous as to consequences. Does the precautionary principle tell us whether or not to build them, even when all precautions as to how and where to build are taken? Does the maximin principle help us? We know for a fact that relying instead, as we still do in many countries, on abundant but non-renewable polluting sources of energy carries serious consequences for personal health and for the environment. They have slowly, quietly and methodically killed and continue killing tens of thousands of people and disabling more. In the long run, the sum of the casualties is likely to be much higher than that of a potential nuclear accident. What is *objectively* less bad, and does it make a difference if we know which? Nuclear plants are built, but some countries are more inclined to employ nuclear energy than others (such as France *versus* Italy). What, then, guides us?

In some cases, such as the one just presented, impulsive fears play a role. The decision on whether or not to build nuclear power facilities is likely to be influenced by the emotional salience of the risk they carry.[7] The Italian Government understood the risks quite well when, after Japan's earthquake and tsunami of 2011, it tried (but failed) to suspend an already scheduled popular referendum severely restricting – if approved – the construction of nuclear facilities. Ninety-four per cent of the voters approved the restriction, an incredible margin of victory clearly higher than those anticipated by opinion polls taken before the tsunami. The emotional salience of risk is another illustration of the availability bias. If emotions are at play, the perceived probability is further boosted. The projected image of a nuclear disaster, let alone actual images, is that of one single, tangible, devastating event. Its damages are concentrated in a specific, recognisable area and affect a specific, recognisable population. In comparison, the innumerable present and cumulative damages, to people and to nature, from the constant use of polluting energy resources are often dispersed as to causes, timing, territories and populations. Therefore, if it is a matter of choosing between the two risks, decision makers and commentators might feel free to ignore the second risk. Its victims die quietly, one at a time, in anonymous hospitals. There is no immediate, spontaneous, diffuse, moralising panic of the type that accompanies an epidemic (not necessarily a pandemic, since a pandemic is endemic). It is a fact that unregulated coal kills more people in the USA than terrorists do. When president Obama remarked on this fact, his opponent in the 2012 presidential elections

---

7. Some incurable or deadly diseases, especially if new, by their nature capture the imagination more than others, even if the others cause more casualties. The former may receive greater research funds.

lost no time in denouncing the assertion as lunacy. Similarly, we (some of us) moralise after mass shootings take place and ask that something be done. In the United States, 243 people were killed in mass shootings between April 1999 (Columbine High School) and August 2012. On average, 30 people a day are also murdered in as many gun attacks (twice as many commit suicide with a gun). The guns are small, ordinary handguns; they are *Saturday Night Specials*, useless for a rampage, yet much more lethal because of their availability and their number. The morning after, every morning after, we do not count, mourn, moralise, ask for action.[8]

To repeat, precisely because of its generally non-finished nature, we can twist the precautionary principle to give our decisions pseudo-scientific authority. We can, consciously or unconsciously, stretch it beyond ordinary meaning. As an occasion for *ad hoc* uses, the principle is objectively unfinished because the cases for which it is invoked are far from clear with regard to all the components that make the risk extreme, as well as to the chances that dealing with one case of risk will trigger other risks. Therefore, subjectivity may succor in affecting when to believe it appropriate, or inappropriate, to call for extreme caution. One particularly significant factor in buttressing subjective appeals to extreme caution is how we narrate the risk (and at times how the risk narrates itself). The most effective, though not the easiest, narrative that may be offered is one that dresses up the risk in moral garb, i.e. one that narrates drastic action against risk as the only or the superior protection against morally unquestionable damage. This removes the need for difficult relative calculations. Moral reasons, when persuasively articulated, manage to rescue, so to say, the precautionary principle from its unfinished nature. They cast and synthesise it as a clear and ultimate obligation, which dispenses with any reflection and afterthought. Instead, when moral reasons are in short supply, the issue of precaution may remain central but will not lend itself to smooth solutions.

Comparing neoliberal risk policies

The section above, and the last paragraph in particular should help clarify why, how, and with what success neoliberal policies justify, for themselves and for others, the treatment of different types of risk. In the case of social risks, I have already argued, perhaps *ad nauseam*, that neoliberal policies tend to contribute to, reinforce and justify more recent extra-political trends transferring the burden of social risks onto those affected by them. I have said little about the justifications of neoliberal policies in regard to ecological risks, with their impact on human health and the environment. I have barely mentioned a new type of risk, in part connected to the former. I am referring to risks brought about by the new biotechnologies and by genetic modifications, affecting Nature as well as the human species. In

---

8. The same availability bias operates in the case of empathic behaviour. We empathise and some of us donate money for surgery that could save the life of 6-year old 'Peggy'. But in order for us to donate money, the life to be saved must have a name, a face and a story suitably offered on prime time. Human empathy is, in this sense, a fickle sentiment.

synthesis, this is my position: neoliberal policies toward social risk are notable for the wilfulness of their objectives and the syncretism of precautionary and moral claims in their defence. Hence, opposition to those policies is also clear; its ethical components are similarly straightforward and secular in nature. They are secular because in the final analysis neoliberalism hashes over issues of liberty and equality that have been with us since the beginning of the work society. As to neoliberalism's approach to the new types of risk, a few premises are in order. Undoubtedly, if there are risks that nowadays present each one of us with not only material but also urgent and profound ethical dilemmas, they are to be found among the new manufactured risks. But, unfortunately, if there are risks that are particularly resistant to clear, possibly shared solutions, they are precisely these same manufactured risks. Their dilemmas touch, no less, upon human life and the life of the planet that is hosting us; upon the way we dispose of our life and that of our planet. At least so far, each answer to the dilemmas carries consequences that are morally ambivalent and divisive to say the least. Considerable medical progress has been made, for instance, in the early diagnosis of diseases that are not curable in their advanced stage, and in the diagnosis of disease proneness. However, early diagnoses of eventually incurable diseases can trigger still unknown immediate risks, such as false positives or the discovery and treatment of other affections ordinarily of no great import. It can be said that the greater the progress in medicine, biotechnologies in particular, the greater the incidence of iatrogenic risks. Similarly, the benefits of genetic modification in agriculture, even when indisputable, clash with claims about their presumed negative impact on personal health. If these claims were proven correct, the moral dilemma would harden. The ethics that distinguish these life domains is one of profound personal identity. Its attention is on what is appropriate, not so much in our mundane relations with our own kind, as in our relation with our body and with the natural world which sustains us. This is why decisions regarding what is to be done about risks of this kind are morally dismaying and disconcerting. Precautionary principles circumventing the moral issue would give us incomplete answers. Moreover, any step we take would be accompanied by a moral warning and, hence, paralysis.

Still, the very fact that we are dealing with ultimately ethical uncertainties offers decision makers the opportunity to make a case for their policies, precisely by betting on the ethical dimension. If the least damage from a maximin calculus is still ethically uncomfortable damage, then what may recommend itself is a new narrative that removes doubts about the ethically correct choice, or reconstructs that ethics; a narrative whose language is not prudentially ordinal (maximin) but binary and incontrovertible – one that calls for commitment. However, this is easier said than done. One decisive obstacle is that even decision makers that like to think of themselves as unbending and consistent in the application of their values, are neither. We all embrace not one but a host of values that, whatever we may think, are neither exclusive of one another nor bendable to positive ordinal calculus. Hence the apparent inconsistency between responses to different risks. Opposition to genetic modification in agriculture may go together with support for medical research employing embryonic stem cells and vice versa. Especially in already advanced agricultures, we may oppose genetic modification because we emphasise, for instance, personal risks over collective economic gains. At the same time, the new cures promised by medical research on stem cells may overshadow, among the same people who oppose genetic modification in agriculture, moral considerations about the destruction of embryos or about eugenetics choices. In the United States, genetic modification in agriculture is, in general, currently more acceptable than in Europe; but opposition to stem cell research is generally greater. What may appear as an inconsistency between single stands has little to do with the vagueness of the precautionary principle, since the latter cannot mould what is decided. [9] Inconsistency in moral stands is not a defect subject to objective correction, it describes the way we are.

Let me now return to comparing neoliberal policies toward different types of risk, by restating first the case of social risks. In their regard, neoliberalism has elaborated an alternative hegemonic narrative, internally coherent and confident, in which recovering the lost values of personal responsibility constitutes the appropriate response to social risks. Neoliberalism reproblematises social risk. It rejects what in the past century was constructed and addressed in collective solidarity as a risk for all society, born from the practices and expectations that industrial society imposes on the workforce and its communities. It flips the old narrative upside down. The true cause of social risk has now been identified in the long-practiced social construct: solidarity. Solidarity is dependency, a drain on the promises of late industrial society and a drain on the autonomy of its members. Neoliberalism offers the ideas and the policies to stop dependency. The project is, however, ambitious and cannot rely on the liberating fiction of government at a distance. It cannot rely on spontaneity; it must rely on an interventionist philosophy and interventionist policies that bear directly on re-education and Foucauldian discipline. Foucault is explicit on this point. In his 1978–79 lectures at the Collège de France, Foucault (2008: 137) argues that neoliberalism is not to be confused

---

9.　There are cases, as we have seen, in which the precautionary principle is invoked on the basis of one-sided, partial or distorted evidence of risk. In the United States, public opinion is divided on the possession of arms and the risks associated with it. Those who favour possession will cite evidence intended to prove that a prowler will not enter a household if he knows that the residents are armed. Those who oppose possession will cite evidence showing that the presence of arms in a household presents risks for the residents. Actually, it is not the statistics that make the case for or against possession (since the data may support both advocates and opponents of possession), but the values that underlie the appeal to selected data. No demonstration that gun possession increases personal safety will convince some people that possession is right (unless, possibly, extreme circumstances are present: the neighbourhood is a high risk area and pretty much everyone has a gun). And if in the final analysis the prevailing danger of arms and arm possession were demonstrated, American advocates of gun possession would appeal to the second amendment of the constitution. The fact that the Supreme Court has recently supported their position with a majority of only five to four, and with the indication of some conditions for restraining possession, does little or nothing to change the minds of those who oppose guns. The same considerations apply to issues like the death penalty, abortion, and other contested social issues.

with *laissez-faire*. On the contrary, the former is a system of perpetual vigilance, activism and interventionism. I should add that this interventionist philosophy is Foucauldian in the harshest sense, in that the neoliberal version lacks the collective and diffuse dimension of discipline, shared *sine ira et studio* (without resentment and zealousness), which Foucault observed in the development and practices of the modern Western state. Neoliberal discipline aims at personal responsibilisation as a necessary premise to the liberation of producers and productive forces from the fetters of the state. It does so by relying on a rational model of individual choice driven by a calculus of incentives and disincentives, presumed to be equally employable by everybody. Further, in constructing solidarity as the true source of individual deresponsibilisation (trained dependency, trained incapacity) and as the foremost danger for the whole society, it adds a dimension of moral appropriateness to its appeal. Two salutary deontologies thus converge in support of the individualisation of social risk: that of personal responsibility and that of a self-steering social order. Together, they should nullify the uncertainties of the precautionary principle.

On matters of social risks, neoliberal rational-political activism merges with the equally active moral component of politically engaged neoconservatism. The resulting synergy gives neoliberalism (as well as neoconservatism) added leverage on a larger public. The two *isms* travel together in a not-so-strange honeymoon. They are still two bodies and two souls as well. Although, at times, the terms neoliberalism and neoconservatism are used interchangeably, the objects of their moralising, the subjects of their reprehension and the solutions they advocate not always coincide. Neoliberalism may not need the backing of moral neoconservatism when it comes to those aspects of the neoliberal agenda that more strictly and harshly reflect a faith, which the various strands of neoconservatism not always share, in the untrammeled resources of the market. However, the cohabitation of neoliberalism and moral neoconservatism is ultimately helped by their shared scepticism toward the capacity of the individual – some classes much more than others – for self-redemption when left without proper guidance. Both hold the unreformed state as indifferent toward individual immorality, and even aiding it (welfarism). Both embrace social engineering as the appropriate response to these predicaments. Morally driven social engineering separates neoliberalism and neoconservatism from their presumptive predecessors: classical liberalism and classical conservatism. I dealt in Chapter Three with the difference between neoliberalism and liberalism; the latter in the European political sense, not in the misleading American sense of social progressivism. As to classical Burkean Conservatism, many of its features are in antithesis to neoconservatism (its anti-enlightenment emphasis on the layering of tradition and the weight of history, community, intermediate bodies, sentiments, and caring; its repudiation of rationality and individualism as cold intellectual constructs not immune from Platonic guidance; its suspicion toward comprehensive innovation; its belief that, although human nature is fallible, its resistance to change is to be respected; its penchant for limits, moderation, and frugality; its respect for status and natural hierarchies; its secularism; its moral and religious tolerance; its Victorian display of outward appearances and manners; its pragmatism; its suspicion of new wealth). However, these features are also in antithesis to neoliberalism. Both neoliberalism and neoconservatism share a confident, subversive project on social issues that morally transcends democratic discourse and deliberation.

Moving at long-last to the neoliberal approach toward new manufactured risks, I would like to treat first ecological and environmental risks, I will then close the chapter by dealing with individual risks stemming from advances in human biotechnologies. A recent study by David Vogel (2012) of policies toward consumer and environmental risks in Europe and the United States reveals an interesting trend. American policies and public opinion were much more risk-averse in the thirty years or so before the nineties, and increasingly less risk-averse afterwards. Europe and progressively integrated European institutions show a reverse, growingly risk-aversion trend. The American trend toward less risk-aversion coincides with the greater grip of neoliberalism that began in the last few years of the past century. Coincidence is not foolproof explanation,[10] but there are some aspects of new environmental risks that may broadly account for that coincidence. I have in mind (a) the fact that major environmental risks are manufactured not by single individuals but by large money-making organisations; and (b) the fact that what science unequivocally tells us about environmental risks and how to address them rubs against neoliberal priorities.

Environmental risks are risks that, if we believe in their presence and in our need and capacity to address them, can only be addressed with a type of policy that fits their collective nature. Environmental risks are a collective bad, collective both in their origins and in their impact. They are so by definition, irrespective of whether they are man-made. Instead, social risks were (until and even before the past century) collective because that had been the way we chose to define, narrate and address them. It does not necessarily follow from the collective nature of environmental risks that remedies will be sought; but it follows that if remedies are sought, it may not seem advisable to leave their adoption and implementation to the discretion of private initiatives. Discretionary action is action dispersed and limited in its effects. In short, there are no uniformly shared incentives for strictly private initiative. Hence, relying on private initiative will leave in place, in the perspective of environmentalists, a tragedy of the commons, where the commons are a fact of nature but the abuse of the commons is tragically manufactured. Environmentalism calls for public initiative and guidance, both of them comprehensive in scope. Given the reach of some environmental risks, invoked action in regard to risks of vast ecological dimensions will easily go beyond the confines of single nation states. All of this is a nightmare for the public-choice market-rational mindset of neoliberalism. Environmentalists' absolutisation of environmental risks rubs against that mindset. The more environmental risks assume a global dimension, the greater neoliberal scepticism

---

10. Has there more recently been anything comparable to the thermonuclear fallout and the pesticide scares of the sixties?

becomes; the stronger their absolutisation, the firmer the neoliberal dismissal of drastic precautionary action. Neoliberalism's market-rational mindset favours micromanagement. Micromanagement is about the here and now; the tangible, calculable present (New Public Management). Micromanagement nullifies history. What we defined as systemic social risks, neoliberalism deconstructs and routinely micromanages as individual market-rational failures. There are no powerful ways of micromanaging environmental risks.

How, then, does neoliberalism respond to environmentalism? It cannot dismiss it with silence, since environmental risks are, after all, part of what defines our risk-aware societies. The first and strongest response is to deny that environmental risks are manufactured. This is more easily achieved, and with greater abandon, when the risks are not localised and contingent but verging on global. The presence of overwhelming evidence to the contrary is no obstacle to denial of the human factor. Evidence, after all, has not been an obstacle to denying the role of untrammelled business and lax government in the 2008 economic recession. Denials may even offer as evidence ludicrous conspiracy theories by consorted world scientists. Nonetheless, like the Big Lie, denials leave a mark in public opinion (Vogel 2012) in the same way in which theories of creationism, which by their nature cannot be disproven, are nevertheless seen by some, authorities and public opinion alike, as something to be thought about on a par with (needless to say, highly questionable) evolutionism. A subsidiary neoliberal response to global climatic changes is to attribute the changes to natural effects. This rules out the need for policies that alter risky human behaviour on a global scale. As to local environmental damages whose causes or remedies involve human action – for instance, regarding local pollution, food safety, energy preservation and energy independence – neoliberalism can seize upon a number of prudential factors against rushing to untested remedies, especially of a drastic nature (1 per cent doctrine). Among the reasons for prudence are: the remedies' performance is uncertain; the amount, the nature and the interplay of changes are not yet known; we are not able to establish if and when a point of no return will be reached; therefore remedies should wait. An additional reason that is usually given for delaying is that the economy cannot afford costs that are likely to negatively affect it. The assertion is advanced with greater authority if the economy is already underperforming, as when a country is trying to recover from a recession. Recovery is hampered while the returns of environmental protection, even when certain, may be neither immediate nor tangible.

The important point is not whether the reservations above have some independent credibility of their own, which they may, but why neoliberalism puts them forward. They are put forward because they follow from what I shall call neoliberalism's market-rational nullification of history. Rushing to drastic measures is resisted not because resistance may make sense but, more fundamentally, because drastic measures require the hand of governments, and empowered governments are tempted to approach environmental risks with an eye that looks beyond immediate cost-benefit accounting. In the improvident hands of empowered governments, costs become unsustainable, almost by definition. And if they are unsustainable, they should not be sustained.

I move now to risks associated with medical and biotechnological advances. These advances impressed me as perfect for fulfilling the ideal-typical neoliberal person's aspiration to a life free of unwanted surprises. Medical and biotechnological advances present risks but, unlike the other risks (which we, if aware, try to avoid), they also allure us with previously unimaginable opportunities. The promises of individual health are more and more promises of man-made health and, short of moral imperatives against some of its means or its ends, habituation to manufactured promises may prevail over consideration of the risks and uncertainties that accompany them. The subjectively prevailing risks are, in our neoliberal minds, not so much the side-risks of medical progress but the lost opportunities stemming from regulating and thus slowing medical progress. Hence, I venture to suggest that, without quite knowing it, neoliberalism – aided by medical progress - has in this regard already fulfilled part of its transformative ambition: the moulding of a human neoliberal prototype. The promises and opportunities are fostered by the expectation of unlimited progress, such as to challenge the inalterable parameters of life, health, ageing and death. A long life, a healthy life, a bionic life, a deservedly enjoyable life (of the leisurely, sporty type depicted in incurably upbeat medical commercials),[11] is something we feel entitled to. The risks associated with the natural flow of life have no objective reason to exist and, since they are potentially reversible, no moral reason either. Neoliberalism as promoter of individual risk prevention has played an indirect, yet important and, when all is said and done, unsurprising role in the development of these expectations. We already know that neoliberal consumers, those who can help themselves, are induced to take individual precautions against their personally constructed risks. The precautions are in keeping with the neoliberal injunction: take care; you are on your own. I have discussed some of these precautions at length in previous chapters. They were mainly about public security, personally pursued; about the pursuit, obsessive at times, of a life absolutely protected from the physical threats or the irresponsible behaviour of others-from-us. Similarly personal have been the insistent quest for products and services which the market advertises as safe and health promoting and the demand for safe public services and infrastructures.

To these expectations of prevention we can now add the ultimate expectation of a physical life bio-medically equipped against the inconveniences of sickness and ageing. What seemed impossible until a few years ago, is being brought close to us by medical science.[12] Contrary to generally more distant attitudes toward

---

11. The legally imposed, interminable spoken list of iatrogenic side-effects that in TV ads accompany the extolling of a newfangled medical drug easily falls on deaf ears: it is too long and monotonous, too hair-raising if taken seriously, and finally unpersuasive against the Norman Rockwell background of newly healthy grandfathers disporting themselves with their grandchildren.

12. When our car or dishwasher gets old, we stop buying replacement parts and buy a new, improved model. We may soon be able to do better with our defective body: we keep it and improve it with bionic tinkering. We will no longer need to buy and implant parts that are usually second-hand and not always durable.

global environmental risks, we tend to perceive all the inconveniences of living that I just described as impending and personal, part of our daily concerns. In all of these cases, risk aversion prevails and demands drastic risk prevention. Here, the neoliberal dream seems to reach near fulfilment. The dream is the creation of the near-perfect neoliberal person, attuned to those aspects of the risk society that should most directly awaken personal initiative: from personal risks to personal aversion to risks, and from this to easy initiative and prevention. As we are induced to act according to the neoliberal code – whether or not we are aware of it, and whether or not it fits our self-image – we are consumed by aversion to personal risks. We are taught to and called to avert them by placing individual freedom of action at the service, above all, of our immunity from the unpleasant and unpredictable within and outside us. Freedom of action is not just at the service of political autonomy. It can now be more importantly and productively at the service of our own privately secured wellbeing. It has now become, as I wrote in Chapter Seven, a human right for utilitarian purposes (Garapon 2012: 67). Thus, we live in an eternal present, where the future is nothing but the safe attendance to our daily selves.

Still, this is not the entire story. We already know that most people, the others-from-us, are not equipped to fulfil the neoliberal role. Personal security is not for them – in fact, it is against them. Also, as consumers of products and services, these others are less protected than we are. They are on the losing side of neoliberalism's dual society. Nor are the others quite in a position to expect a physical life immune from sickness and ageing. One of the reasons for this is that, when it comes to medical services, neoliberalism's priority is not their quality but their privatisation.[13] Thus, with the unintentional help of medical progress, neoliberalism's dual society is reminiscent of science fiction on the creation of a master race.

Dualism aside, how will we, who mostly live on the winning side, adjust to what Robert Castel calls a life in which nothing untoward happens (Castel 1991: 289)? If this is the measure of happiness, one scenario could be a depoliticised utopia, sponsored by the pipedreams described above. Orwell comes to mind. A second scenario is equally anguishing; something closer to a soporific neoliberal fiction than an Orwellian nightmare. If nothing happens, tedium may set in, the tedium that eventually assails the conventionally happy protagonist of the movie *The Truman Show*. He has been living since birth in a TV-staged utopian city of peaceful ordinariness; but only those watching the show know it. Exit, in Albert Hirschman's (1970) sense, will eventually ensue when the protagonist becomes uneasy and goes after the truth. A third scenario, one amply described by Robert Castel, is worth reporting at length,

---

13. This, however, cannot by itself explain why, while the life expectancy of non-Hispanic Caucasians of both genders without a high school degree has fallen in recent years, that of Hispanic and black people with equal levels of education has gone up. According to scholarly research reported in the *New York Times* of 20 September 2012, among the least educated Americans, white women have lost five years of life expectancy since 1990, and white men have lost three years.

The modern ideologies of prevention are overarched by a grandiose technocratic rationalising dream of absolute control of the accidental, understood as the irruption of the unpredictable. In the name of this myth [...], they construct a mass of new risks which constitute so many new targets for preventive intervention [...] Thus, a vast hygienist utopia plays on the alternate registers of fear and security, inducing a delirium of rationality, an absolute reign of calculative reason and a no less absolute prerogative of its agents, planners and technocrats, administrators of happiness for a life to which nothing happens. (Castel 1991: 289)

A happy life where nothing happens or a life of repetitive obsessions and unquenched anxieties? It could be the same thing. Eric Hoffer (1902–1983), San Francisco longshoreman and philosopher, said it best: 'The search for happiness is one of the chief sources of unhappiness'.

A few months ago our residential block held meetings to organise itself against the foreseeable ravages of a major Bay Area earthquake. Most of our neighbours are now better equipped than before, indeed, obsessively equipped, against any and all consequences of a major seismic event. The episode reminded me of our obsession with risk. Nonetheless, my family is now obsessively equipped, ready to upgrade, and apprehensive about the few neighbours who are not equipped (the closer to our household, the greater the apprehension).

Such is the promise of neoliberalism.

I would like to close this chapter with one reflection. It will sound like science fiction but it is not. It could open a Pandora's box, but I shall keep the box's lid ajar. I wrote above, and I quote, 'The promises of individual health are more and more the promises of man-made health and, short of moral imperatives against some of its means or ends, habituation to manufactured promises may prevail [...]'. But what about the moral imperatives? Are they there? Do they carry weight? Some may be bogus but not all are bogus. For some, their time has not come. Bogus or not, present or potential, the neoliberal beneficiaries of unlimited medical progress, living as they do in an eternally shielded present, tend to be less than sensitive to those moral imperatives, or unaware of their existence. But that infinite present, perennially and self-assuredly equal to itself, is a fiction of their (our) neoliberal mind.[14] It will take time, but once the fiction is uncovered, neoliberal man will be

---

14. It is also a fiction in which the neoliberal mind can indulge because of its elective affinity with another fiction, that of a Gradgrind-like all-gathering, all-quantifying and therefore all-knowing Internet Mind, as, for instance, well represented by the Quantified Self movement (*quantifiedself. com*). Here is another example among many of the promises of ever-present, ever-available comprehensive web-knowledge: Gordon Bell, Microsoft engineer and manager, and renowned Internet guru, whose often cited books carry such titles as *Total Recall* and *Your Life, Uploaded,* has created a personal, fully-documented 'lifelogging' website that yields him, in his own words, 'enhanced self-insight, the ability to relive his own life in Proustian detail (!?), the freedom to memorise less and think creatively more, and even a measure of *earthly immortality* by being cyberised' (as quoted by Morozov 2013: 270, [my emphasis]). Here, then, courtesy of neoliberalism and the Internet, is the instant *über*-utopia: squared immortality, fully transcending the evanescent *Madeleine*.

defenceless and without guidance, short of what I would call a moral conversion, i.e. an exit from his neoliberal self. Consider the following scenario from Hans Jonas. The scenario is implausible, but its implausibility best displays the ultimate fiction by which we live at our own risk:

> To take the extreme (not that it will ever be obtained): if we abolish death, we must abolish procreation as well, for the latter is life's answer to the former, and so we would have a world of old age with no youth, and of known individuals with no surprises [...] [The wisdom of mortality] grants us the eternally renewed promise of the freshness, immediacy and eagerness of youth, together with the supply of otherness [...] This ever renewed beginning, which is only to be had at the price of ever repeated ending, may well be mankind's hope, its safeguard against lapsing into boredom and routine, its chance of retaining the spontaneity of life [...] So it could be that [...][the] gift of science to man, the partial granting of his oldest wish – to escape the curse of mortality – turns out to be to the detriment of man [...] [T]he promised gift raises questions that [...] must be dealt with ethically and by principle and not merely by the pressure of interest. (Jonas 1973)

This is all.[15]

---

15. José Saramago's novel (*Death with Interruptions*, Boston: Houghton Mifflin Harcourt, 2008) is an inventive rendition of the grotesque consequences, in a not-so-fictional country, of Death's decision to take a break. Many of them are close to Jonas' anticipations. In *Gulliver's Travels*, the inhabitants of the nation of Luggnagg are immortal. However, when they age, which they do miserably, they become legally dead in the eyes of the law (no property, no employment, etc.). That is one way to prevent them from owning and controlling everything. Not a nice solution, not for the aged, not for society, and not when compared to Jonas' comforting, long-tested alternative.

Chapter Eight

Challenges to Neoliberalism?

Précis

I began this essay by drawing on great theorisations. To start with, I relied on Max Weber and Michel Foucault. With their lesson in mind, I revisited the art of government of the great democracies of the past century, and prepared myself to address the present predicaments of that art. I might have started with other theorisations, but I was enticed by the possible convergence in the thought of two scholars so different in academic formation and approaches. Placing them side-by-side allowed me to offer a combined reading, from both the top and the bottom, of the modern state as the most eventful experiment in the art of governing ourselves on a large scale. In my reading, the Weberian rationality from the top exhibited by modern state institutions expands into Foucauldian *gouvernementalité*; that is, into an anthropological condensation of modernity's teeming techniques of public and individual conduct. With the help of Martin Lipset, the convergence of Weber with Foucault has then provided me with a better understanding of what I called government of the social with the social, supported over time by shared public-private languages and conducts.

At the end of this revisitation, I devoted Chapters Three, Four and Five to the uncertainties of the present, to ask whether the current predicaments of government and society, and the coming apart in particular of state-sponsored solidarity against social risks, signal a stress in the metal of Weber's rationality cage (the cage within which, with Foucauldian discipline, the governing of the social had been operating). Thus formulated, the question I asked remained at a rather abstract level. This is not an apology. This is the level to which Weber and Foucault took me. Though moving from different perspectives – Weber from removed disenchantment; Foucault from anthropological testimony – the two thinkers helped me understand the terrain of ideal and material solidarity combined with formal discipline that state and society came to share. And they helped me understand the nature of the present predicament as a yielding of that shared terrain. It is true that the modern state is less defined by the material content of its actions and policies than by the stable formal rationality of its actions. As my old colleague Gianfranco Poggi is fond of repeating in several of his works on the modern state, the modern state is rather taken to pursuing a cascade of 'contingent, open-ended endeavours'. But, as if responding to Poggi, Colin Gordon goes back to the birth of the modern state and notes,

[...] [the] problem of calculating detailed actions appropriate to an infinity of unforeseeable and contingent circumstances is met by the creation of an exhaustively detailed knowledge of the governed reality of the state itself extending [...] to touch the existences of its individual members. The police state is also termed the 'state of prosperity'. (Gordon 1991:10)

State security, that is, state endurance, depended on prosperity. Prosperity as a means in the service of the state eventually gave way, as we saw in Chapter Two, to prosperity in the interest of its citizens and was inseparable from solidarity.

After analysing the lapsing of solidarity/prosperity, I progressively relied in the rest of the chapters upon the burgeoning literature on the risk society. It helped me establish analytical continuity as I moved from the past solidarity against social risks to the present insecurities in regard to old and new risks. There are, however, other aspects of the risk society literature, stressed by some of its contributors, that prefigure the rise of a popular challenge to neoliberalism's erosion of societal cohesiveness and dialogue. Some of the literature is inclined to see in the widespread attainment of risk awareness the premise and promise of communal resistance to societal erosion. But the literature is short of empirical support and normatively questionable.

Scepticism, which I will now justify, about that literature's promises will still leave me with another, more mainstream challenge to neoliberalism. But, as I will argue in closing this chapter, mainstream does not mean winning.

Risk awareness and critical participation

I begin with what I shall call for the sake of convenience the Rose conjecture. Nikolas Rose, has in mind neoliberalism's theorisation of responsible individual empowerment through governing at a distance, when he critically conjectures,

> The formulae of liberal government that I have termed 'advanced' are much more significant than the brief flowering of neo-liberal political rhetorics may indicate [...]. Although strategies of welfare sought to govern through society, 'advanced' liberal strategies of rule ask whether it is possible to govern without governing society, that is to say, to govern through the regulated and accountable choices of autonomous agents – citizens, consumers, parents, employees, managers, investors – and to govern through intensifying and acting upon their allegiance to particular 'communities'. (Rose 1996: 61)

As formulated, the conjecture has at first its own attractiveness. It offers a more promising perspective on the paths that governing at a distance may leave open. It envisions a system of self-government structured around the diffuse functional self-representation of societal and economic interests. As such, it actually has its own historical intellectual pedigree, with examples and elaborations within democracies but also within non-democracies. Nonetheless, it remains a conjecture, one that (at present) rubs against the grim reality of governing at a distance that I have presented, with the help of other scholars, in this essay. Therefore, I will read what Rose conjectures as a utopia against an existing order. As a utopia, it does not deliver because it promises what is not yet there: a newly ordering paradigm. As a utopia, a non-place, it must confront a space that neoliberalism occupies and, engaged as neoliberalism now is in attending to its mode of governing, is not ready to vacate. It is a disingenuous play on words on my part, but that utopia must confront a dystopia, in fact a despotic dystopia. A neoliberal dystopia has something robustly present about itself that a future-oriented utopia does not have. Further, it is possible to conceive and document government without society (dictatorship). But a society without government, governing itself smoothly from the ground up, is (at least today) neither documentable nor conceivable. I find it similarly difficult to believe that, in terms of representativeness, legitimacy, effectiveness, accountability and responsiveness, such a self-governing society, were it ever to take shape, could be a model of democratic government.[1] The 'Rose conjecture' seems to resolve these problems when it depicts self-governing functional groups as regulated and held accountable in their governing. But regulated by whom, and accountable to whom?

In regard to the conjecture, I cited Rose and could cite other contributors to the literature on risk society. They tend to be liberal in the American sense; they tend to share, albeit with reservations and distinctions, a view of self-government as a promising reaction to the neoliberal dystopia, whose wishful nature could only be confounded by a difficult constructivist test. As a wish and a promise, self-government from the bottom up sounds captivating. It evokes the enlightened ideal of an autonomous public sphere capable of dealing with both the social costs of the market and the intrusions of the state. Formulated as a mere wish, it needs no empirical proof. However, when it is presented as an alternative reality still under human construction, it must pass harsher tests. What are the resources that can be displayed for the construction of an alternative self-governing order, and how do they stack up against the reality of neoliberal government? The resources are largely subjective. Their subjectivism as embodied in the Rose conjecture is of a particular type.[2] It is programmatic and exhortative; it relies on the virtues of a new way of knowing, of critical thought that teaches and liberates us by providing reflexive personal awareness. It is, in essence, discursively performative.[3] There is nothing inherently illusory with transformative discourses. They can in principle

---

1. Unless, of course, one is ready to embrace the latest bromide: the global, liberating potential of the so-called Internet revolution, which is single-handedly supposed to be unleashing, as you read this footnote, openness and transparency, and with it a popular insurgence from the ground up (parties and government are no longer needed). A caustic analysis of this latest bromide and its questionable academic pretences is most recently offered by Evgeny Morozov (2013).

2. Subjectivism is a broad label embracing a number of culturally driven approaches to knowledge, such as discursivism, constructivism, critical theory, reflexivism. Strydom (2002) offers an extensive analysis of them. I am not interested in criticizing the subjectively driven optimism of specific contributors to the study of risk society. I am merely suggesting a generally prudential reading of their optimism, as for instance the optimism adumbrated in Rose's quote above.

3. Performative utterances are statements whose mere expression intends to transform what it describes. Neoliberalism at its best combines the subversive with the discursive.

remove the hurdles, subjective but also objective, that interfere with collective action. But in our case, collective mobilisation is a tall-order. It demands the horizontally diffuse engagement of a large spectrum of citizens that neoliberalism is already busy dispersing and isolating. How do the same actors that neoliberalism is intent on bending to its narrative possibly become the protagonists in the construction of an alternative order?

We know that neoliberalism's bending narrative is debilitating and in fact disempowering for most. The individual assumption of risks relies, according to neoliberalism, on the postulates of the positive theory of public choice. According to this theory, choice is an individual rational calculus of costs and benefits. The theory's parsimony, stemming from neoclassical economics, postulates a free and spontaneous calculus. However, we have already seen how the individual assumption of risk under neoliberal sponsorship is in reality neither free nor exactly inborn. If risk assumption occurs, it occurs because of the dour and firm *aut aut* with which we are left when the collective coverage of risk is either removed or under threat of removal. There are other reasons for doubting the promises of a spontaneous, individually liberating calculus. The market as the new arena for dealing with risk is not only imposed, it also habitually operates on an uneven playing field where suppliers have the upper hand. Undoubtedly, market-driven persuasion is buttressed by moral-sounding injunctions: know and tow the line, take care of your health, take care of your needs, watch and protect yourself, your choices and conducts will be the measure of your reward or punishment. However, the injunctions are morally disingenuous and unpersuasive, given that most 'consumers' find themselves disadvantaged by the nature of the market of costs and benefits. Finally, the few who, possibly under duress, adjust to the 'you-are-on-your-own' neoliberal injunctions, often end up by living, to borrow Garapon's strong words, 'a pavid and calculating individualism' (Garapon 2012: 164). More mildly put, 'they bowl alone' (Putnam 1995). It follows that the algebraic sum of the individual utilities and disutilities of each un-free decision as to whether and how to seek protection from risk, produces, at best, utilities dressed in pseudo-Benthamite garb, ones in which the 'happiness' of a minority sustains itself at the expense of a majority. But is that happiness genuine, one that simply and virtuously reflects our nature as a utilitarian calculator? I do not believe so. Rather, the neoliberal conviction that we are motivated by the utilitarian calculus creates, with the help of appropriate policies, utilitarian incentives and disincentives intended to fulfil the neoliberal prophecy.[4] Thus, an imposed calculus miraculously mutates into a spontaneous individual and social value. Before the advent of neoliberalism those individualising incentives and disincentives were largely absent. Instead, the systems that attended to the collective coverage of risk

---

4. For some people the calculus may pay off. For instance, thanks to medical progress, some people may on their own be able to better and more regularly control their health, by employing new gismos that constantly monitor, let us say, the medical effects of their feeding habits. But the payoff remains personal, limited to some, and utilitarian. It is no substitute for stricter monitoring of the food industry. Yet it may soften public demands for such monitoring.

constructed risk as a generally dispersed phenomenon, imputed to nobody and covered by the community. The costs of coverage were universal and therefore latent. Once risk and coverage become matters of personal responsibility, risk is no longer dispersed, its costs no longer latent but charged to those who carry it. And a number of individuals, each one of them left to his own resources, whatever they are, do not constitute a political community. How then can they be recruited to build the communities that Rose posits?

Also, Rose specifies that his communities will govern through regulated and accountable choices. What does this mean? I am reminded of the fact that neoliberal policies on risk have already given birth to a sequence of regulations, devices, techniques and organisational forms that should presumably ease and encourage the adoption of individual practices of risk coverage. One example among many of the tools that neoliberalism employs for this purpose is the self-righteously named 'Patient's Bill of Rights', sponsored at the end of the nineties by President Clinton's Democratic administration. The bill covered a whole set of patients, families, communities, professionals, agencies and institutions having title to its protection. Since resorting to the protection of the bill is largely in the hands of the consumer, and since the consumer is defined by and credited for his own initiatives, it would seem appropriate to speak of this and other examples as genuine instances of governing at a distance, by personally empowering the consumer to protect himself.[5] It sounds like soft governing, with discretion. But the bill still addresses risk protection as a matter of marketing and contracts. It is one thing to have legal title to protection under the bill, another to be actually willing and able to make use of it (Schlesinger 2005).[6]

In addition, in cases other than the Patient's Bill of Rights, consumers' presumed incentives to take the initiative are often neither discreet nor discretionary. Rather, they are imposed under duress. As we have seen when citing Béatrice Hibou (2012), governing at a distance consists in the activation and tuning of a cascade of rules, standards, monitoring, audits, budgeting, optimisations and cost

---

5. Even assuming individual empowerment, we should not confuse this turning of the citizen into a consumer with the emphasis that the early twentieth century Progressive Movement placed on the defence of the consumer as citizen. Progressivism advocated active civic republicanism against the incapacitating invasion of burgeoning private monopolies. It aimed at the public protection of the individual not against but in the name of the social and the community. In the Progressive Movement's communitarian spirit, the consumer is a joiner; under neoliberalism, he is not.

6. This is the more so in view of the fact that, as it stands, the Patient's Bill of Rights does not provide the patient with what Thaler and Sunstein (2008) call nudges. The two authors have devoted a hefty volume to nudges as a form of libertarian paternalism, designed, among other things, to help supersede decisional inertia. Inertia is especially likely when the choices offered, free-market style, to the individual consumer are many and complex and the comparative advantage of any choice uncertain. Nudges are paternalistic in that they ease the consumer's identification of their preferred choices; they are libertarian in that they leave the consumer free to decide. What would make the guidance of nudges essential, if not sufficient, in the Patient's Bill of Rights is the fact that the patient must find his way in a veritable maze of imposed rules, relations and practices intended to hold together a health coverage system designed for private profit. Without a nudge, patient's decisions under the bill remain free, but his choices are most likely suboptimal.

analyses. They are activations initiated and verified by government, imposing on the consumer a spectrum of conducts and compliances. In the introduction to their edited volume, Barry *et al.* write,

> Paradoxically, neoliberalism, alongside its critique of the deadening consequences of the 'intrusion of the State' into the life of the individual, has none the less provoked the invention and/or deployment of a whole array of organisational forms and technical methods in order to extend the field within which a certain kind of economic freedom might be practiced in the form of personal autonomy, enterprise and choice. (Barry *et al.* 1996: 10)

In an edited volume on neoliberalism in Europe, the editor, Bruno Jobert comments,

> Le néo-libéralisme promu au nome du retrait de l'Etat apparaît ainsi comme un outil de réaffirmation du politique. Il signe moins la mort de l'Etat qu'un nouveau style d'action publique moins dépendant des grands partenaires sociaux, moins encline à produire directement des services ou à organiser la redistribution des ressources. Dans cette démarche [...] les collectivités politiques se veulent être moins des acteurs que des arbitres du jeu social. (Jobert 1994: 20)[7]

Jobert describes neoliberal political collectivities, meaning neoliberal public institutions, as arbiters more than actors. But what does arbitration involve? Both Jobert and Barry *et al.* suggest that there is little clearly liberating about this new government role. As an arbiter, neoliberal government sets the rules that guide what has been called a new contractualism. New contractualism is in turn extolled as an effective setting for self-regulating practices. But precisely what is it that the self of self-regulation refers to? Are the regulations self-imposed, and is the self a reflexive self, is it inwardly-directed? Or do the regulations step in to dictate the conduct of the self? In the Foucauldian discipline that marks the classical state the distinction does not exist, and the question has no reason to exist either. Today, the opposite is the case. In a 1971 TV debate between Foucault and Noam Chomsky, the latter expressed his hope in the advent of a kind of *anarcho-syndicalism*, by which he meant a society constituted by a confederation of free, grassroots associations. Foucault rejoined, (author's transcription from the conversation as registered on YouTube)

> À vouloir tout de suite donner le profile et la formule de la société future sans avoir bien fait la critique de tous les rapports de violence politique qui s'exercent dans notre société, on risque de les laisser se reconstituer même

---

7. Thus neoliberalism in the name of retreat from government turns out to be a tool for reaffirming the primacy of the political. Rather than signaling the death of the state, it signals a new style of public action less dependent on the major social partners, less inclined to furnish direct services or to organise resource distribution. By this approach [...] political collectivities aim at being arbiters rather than actors in the social game.

à travers des formes aussi nobles, apparemment aussi pures que celles du syndicalisme anarchique.[8]

At this point, I am compelled to repeat myself. In the neoliberal positive-choice vision, the only reflexive self-regulation that is abstractly conceivable would be that of the *homo oeconomicus*, who enters into individual, voluntary exchange relations. Such relations, inscribed in a hypothetically free market, are theorised as working to the benefits of all involved. Whether or not they do, self-regulation is in this case something automatic, neither a precondition nor even a precautionary intention. There is instead nothing spontaneous to self-regulation when it is a precondition or a precaution; when its burden is meant to fall on citizens; when these citizens are not summoned to contribute to a shared public good, but enjoined in its absence to protect themselves; or when they are enjoined to be free.

It is true – to sum up the last few paragraphs – that the view of the individual as a free agent was born with modern society. His/her unmooring was the product of secularisation in the forms of existence, in the family, in the world of work, in the community. I premise that there would be nothing *per se* natural, or commendable, or commendable because natural, in a return to the origins. At any rate, claims notwithstanding, what we are presently witnessing, courtesy of neoliberalism, is far from a natural return to those origins; one that, by finally putting a stop to the Long Twentieth Century's digression, accelerates history by conflating regress with progress. Personally, I have presented the acceleration as the manifestation of a neoliberal, subversive, non-traditional performative narrative. As is the case with other winning narratives, that of neoliberalism has proven itself resourceful in offering an intentional reading of new realities which, if left to themselves, would look to us like 'one damn thing after another'. Neoliberalism's is a narrative that breaks with and actively reverses the narrative and the achievements of the Long Twentieth Century. With this, I come to my closing point. It seems imprudent to announce the advent now, in answer to neoliberalism but also in answer to the Long Twentieth Century, of yet another narrative, a reflexive re-reading of modernity that emancipates us from both the uncertainties and the disciplines of modernity, past and present. At best, whether such a critical re-reading will stir emancipation can be taken as a conjecture worthy of attention. Before turning it into a verifiable hypothesis, the first task is to document who is re-reading, how many are doing so, and the contents and diversities of such re-readings. As it now stands, the conjecture remains irrefutable because, in Popper's sense of the term, it is formulated with a vagueness (not yet a hypothesis) that impedes confutation. Mapping the arenas where re-readings are occurring (I am not denying their existence) is essential

---

8. To try and submit the profile and formula of the society of the future without first offering a firm critique of all the relations of political violence that mark our own society is a risky affair. We risk allowing the reconstitution of those relations even through the noble, apparently pure guise of anarcho-syndicalism. (Available: http://www.youtube.com/watch?v=8OUkztFhUeI accessed 31 October 2013)

because the arenas are radically new and untested. The historical, discursive and deliberative arenas have been marginalised by neoliberalism's preference for efficient accounting. The arenas envisioned by the Rose conjecture prefigure the construction of discursive and deliberative arenas that break with neoliberalism, but also break with the historical ones.

I close the section by contrasting the theses of two authors. The contrast bears on whether spaces for a renewal of community action exist today. Speaking of the United States, but with other countries in mind, Lawrence Friedman (2002) describes contemporary society as horizontal, open, connected, wired, and ready to question authority and hierarchies, in government, family, school, professions, and religion. He adds, 'A horizontal society is a society of individuals – and individualists. People in society are taught, and come to believe that they have the right and the power to construct a life, a meaning, an identity for themselves as unique individuals' (Friedman 2002: 240). Individuals in a horizontal society, Friedman continues, are in the position to build egalitarian relationships and expect 'total justice'. There are two ways of reading Friedman's assertions. One is to take them as a series of tautologies, which hang together by definition, i.e. this is what a horizontal society of independent individuals is all about. If so, there is nothing wrong with the tautology. Another way is to take the assertions apart. The assertion that we live in a horizontal and wired society may be correct, but the rest does not follow and in fact there is no reason why it should follow. In what seems to me to be an implicit rebuttal of this second reading, Friedman takes into consideration Putnam's (1995) *bowling alone* perspective. Putnam does not question that we live in a horizontal society, a levelling society where everybody is instantly wired to everyone else, rather, he emphasizes it. But he is also intent in documenting the role that this condition exercises on the atomisation and insulation of our lives as members of tangible, lived-in communities. At the beginning of his volume, Friedman counters, 'Putnam's facts and figures can be (and have been) questioned but I feel he has nonetheless put his finger on a real phenomenon. However, whether it is a problem – a source of social malaise – is another story' (Friedman 2002: 26). The narrative that seizes Friedman's attention is not the malaise accompanying the waning of social capital that Putman reports[9] but rather something more resembling the Rose conjecture. Closer instead to the thrust of this chapter and to Putnam's concerns is what Giuseppe De Rita writes in a leading Italian daily on the ungluing of today's horizontal societies,

> We live next to each other but we do not connect. We all live as solitary components of a society that has lost arenas, occasions and opportunities of social integration [...] We remain molecules that can get close, but do not merge and bind. (*Corriere della Sera,* 8 June 2008 [my translation])

---

9. However, in Putnam's analysis of the sources of societal fragmentation and the waning of social capital there is no room for the neoliberal policies in regard to social risks and solidarity or for the transformations in markets, the world of work and the family. Margaret Somers writes, 'I believe [Putnam's] use of the social capital concept is misapplied and wrongheaded. He excludes the entire spectrum of the very institutions of governance, rights, and power without which civil society could not be sustained against the corrosive effects of unregulated markets' (Somers 2008: 235).

A few days later he adds,

More fears than hopes. This is the collective-psychological noose that strangles a society pervaded today by increasing fears, worries, anxieties of every type [...] The prevailing motto seems to be, I hope I can make it – an unpromising motto in terms of commitments to the future and the new. (*Corriere della Sera*, 30 June 2008 [my translation])

Citing De Rita does not disprove Friedman (or the Rose conjecture). Proving or disproving is not the ordinary function of citations. I cite De Rita at this point, following the chapter on the new risks and new risk aversions, because I found his juxtaposition of societal atomisation with growing social anxieties intriguing. In that chapter, I similarly juxtaposed neoliberal man with the individual obsession with risk aversion. In this perspective, Friedman's reference to the spirited demands for total justice in a horizontal society acquires a totally different, bitter, fearful and resentful flavour. It reminds me of the changes in criminal justice, policing and self-policing discussed in Chapter Five. Similarly, distrust of authority, described by Friedman as a positive feature of a horizontal, open society calls to mind the role of neoliberalism in feeding distrust toward public institutions (government is the problem, starve the state). As to distrust toward the authority of social institutions (family, school and so on), I am not equipped to discuss whether they have common roots, and where distrust toward public institutions would fit in the whole. However, in regard to the family and its authority, I refer to Richard Sennett's study (1998) showing how the corrosion of professional character (don't commit yourself, think short-term, don't get involved) in the new world of flexible mobile workers may reflect negatively on the cohesion of their families. For instance, it may erode the worker's exercise of family authority by the example of his professional commitment to a community of co-workers, because that community and that commitment no longer exist.

Third narrative, 'Third Way', neither?

I have described the Rose conjecture as a rough hypothesis, a utopia, an aspiring third narrative. True, there are many signs that a new activism of the type imagined by Rose, an activism from the ground up and diffuse (spontaneous, associational, communitarian, consultative, *movimentista*, participatory, NGO-like), is emerging in many contexts, national and international. I suggested in the previous section the need for a thorough mapping of these arenas as a first step in giving substance to the conjecture. In this, the last section of the chapter, I wish to advance quite a different point. In a vacuum of other democratic institutions, in itself inconceivable, the Rose conjecture could not do a democratic job. Without a comprehensive institutional context that is nationally and locally representative, what special expectations could we possibly entertain as to the effectiveness of a series of policies, aimed for instance at class risks, issued by mere hypothesis from territorially or functionally specific autonomous agents? Active, sensitive and reflexive as those agents may be, their closeness to the interests they serve is not a foolproof, intuitive advantage for other communities or even for their own. If activism is locally rooted and functionally specific, how could its agents deal in isolation with issues of territorial, social and functional inequalities and with discrepancies stemming from their isolation? In the absence of attention to such issues, and to the way in which they must be unavoidably addressed within the broader institutional context in which the agents move, root and branch democracy remains an unfinished academic construct.

What are conceivable and worth considering are the formal-institutional and policy contexts within which the conjecture could best operate. One such institutional context already exists and is operative, after a fashion. It is labelled by its intellectual promoter (Giddens 1998) as *The Third Way* (he was not the first one to use the term). But the Third Way is not a third narrative; it does not re-problematise. It is third in time, but is stuck between two narratives: the neoliberal, ascending and the social-democratic, descending. How hospitable for the Rose conjecture can this positioning really be? As a brand of political thought, the Third Way has been pilloried as a mish mash of ill-digested proposals and second-hand theorisations, masking a make-do surrender to neoliberalism. Others take it for what it wants to be: an effective answer to neoliberalism that, by combining the new realities of the market with the permanent realities of the social, and by opening in particular to the social role of communities, supersedes the state welfarism of the old left. In politics, the most distinguished embodiments of the Third Way are President Clinton's Democratic administration and Tony Blair's Labour Government. It is not without reason that both of them followed the two most innovative neoliberal governments at the time, respectively that of Ronald Reagan and Margaret Thatcher. Giddens (2000) has devoted a volume in defence of the Third Way and in rebuttal to its most severe critics. In my view, it is not necessary to embrace all the criticisms in order to recognise the limits of the Third Way, in general and as host to the Rose conjecture. As a host to the latter, the Third Way does offer some clear advantages. It stresses localism, voluntarism, social networks, devolution, and the alliance of government with a renewed 'big society'. But there are limits , and the limits are inherent. They have little or nothing to do with the fact that the Third Way politics embraced by the Blair/Brown and Clinton governments was only a parenthesis, interrupted by the return to power of neoliberal governments. Following his first manifesto, Giddens had felt vindicated by the victories of Clinton and Blair. He chided his critics as follows,

> Almost everywhere, at least for the moment, conservatism is in retreat. The rise of Third Way politics is partly a reaction to this situation, but has also to some extent helped bringing it about [...] Third Way politics will be the point of view with which others will have to engage. (Giddens 2000: vi–vii)

The limits of the Third Way do not reside in the electoral defeat of its proponents, they reside elsewhere. They have to do with what the Third Way is really all about, and what it proposes to accomplish. They are found in its essence as a way of governing stuck between two contrasting narratives. I wrote that the Third Way is devoted to the creation of a big society, and devoted it was. However, devotion to the big society is not exclusive of the Third Way. Ironically, the term was officially used by the Conservative Government that, in 2010, replaced Gordon Brown's Labour Government. In today's conservative England, that devotion remains at best in the realm of unfulfilled promises.[10] Giddens took solace in the electoral victories of Blair and Clinton. But few elections are, to use an old term from American electoral studies, realigning elections. Rare are the governments that usher in a new narrative. I just said that the Third Way falls in between two narratives. More precisely, despite its aspirations, it is an accommodation to the still-dominant logic of the neoliberal narrative. I rely on the wisdom of Stephen Skowronek's *The Politics Presidents Make* (1993, 1997) and *Presidential Leadership in Political Time* (2008, 2011) to make my case. The central lever in Skowronek's historical-systematic survey of presidential power in America is what he calls political time. The political time of American history is signally marked by 'reconstructive elections', i.e. elections that, as a regime hits a dead end, bring about dramatic changes in governing parties and governing policies. They usher in a new regime. There have been very few such changes, so few that they can be counted on the fingers of one hand (1800, 1828, 1860, 1932, 1980); so few as to deserve being called historic. As Skowronek unfolds their record, over time each regime exhibits very similar patterns of endurance. Endurance is less smooth and more complex than one would expect from the positive feedback effects that Paul Pierson theorises in his *Politics in Time* (2004). Endurance carries increasing over-time tensions. This accounts for similarly occurring variations in the style and performance of the successive presidents of each regime, as well as in the nature of the challenge to the regime brought about by the election of an opposition president.

Of interest for my analysis is Skowronek's documentation and explanation of the reasons why opposition presidents very rarely usher in a new regime. More often, they are, as Skowronek labels them, Third Way presidents, whose pedigree is rooted in culturally defeated regime (one example is president Clinton and the Great Society liberal regime that Reagan had successfully demonised). These presidents preempt the still incumbent regime by selectively borrowing from it, because they are unwilling/unable to reach back to a previously glorious past, or forward to something totally new and no longer indebted to old narratives. President Clinton put preemption succinctly and unabashedly when, in 1991, he declared his intent to run for the presidency ('Neither liberal nor conservative but both and different'), and when, in his 1997 second inaugural speech, he stated, 'Government is not the problem, and government is not the solution' (Skowronek 2008: 106). In fact the policies of his administration have been less notable for their equidistance from liberalism and conservatism than for their effort to prove

---

10. In the remaining pages of the chapter I use the terms conservative and liberal because these are the terms employed by politicians and by many analysts. However, the conservatism to which they refer is not of the common or garden variety. It is neoliberalism. This helps explain the present political polarisation, the main agents of polarisation, and the debility of the Third Way response.

themselves preemptive with respect to the regime which Reagan, 'the great repudiator', inaugurated and his successor swore fealty to. Among the Clintonian policies that are most revealing of preemption are welfare to workfare, which in fact does carry a preemptive name ('Personal Responsibility and Work Opportunities Reconciliation Act'); NAFTA; Don't Ask Don't Tell and Defence of Marriage Acts; support of the death penalty; the Deficit Reduction and Balanced Budget acts; the Crime Bill Act; the Community Police Officers Act; and the Patients' Bill of Rights. 'Historically', Skowronek concludes, 'no Third Way has outlasted the president who articulated it' (Skowronek 2008: 108).

As I was completing the last draft of this chapter, Barak Obama had just been elected to a second term as President of the United States. As Skowronek described his tenure before reelection, 'Obama is a second-round opposition leader pressing the critique of the old regime and probing for reconstructive possibilities [...]' (Skowronek 2011: 193). Obama's first election, according to Skowronek, was not a reconstructive one. Thanks to his personal qualities, but infinitely more so as a result of the political time he inherited, he proved a moderate president in immoderate times; another preemptive leader. Obama inherited the political time of President W. Bush. Bush had proved to be the perfect embodiment of the extremism that characterises what Skowronek calls orthodox innovators, that is, presidents that inherit a founder's regime. In addition, that extremism was successfully pursued by the Republican Party in opposition to Obama. This accounts for the policy constrictions Obama was saddled with.[11] It equally accounts for why his signature legislation, healthcare reform, is largely based on previous conservative ideas and proposals and, though highly regulated, preserves its private nature. Will his second term prove different? I will take up the question at the end of my concluding chapter. Do not hold your breath.

---

11. Written by two scholarly analysts of Congressional politics, known for their cordial bipartisanship as much as for their expertise, Thomas Mann and Norman Ornstein's *Even Worse than It Looks: How the American constitutional system collided with the new politics of extremism* (2012) offers the best comprehensive analysis of the unprecedented obstructionism successfully practiced by the Republican opposition in Congress, and outside.

Chapter Nine

The Future? Ask Me Later

I closed the last chapter with the promise of resuming my reflections on the future of neoliberalism in the United States. Before doing so, I wish to explain at some length, so as to protect my reputation, why my expectations regarding the endurance of neoliberalism should be taken with a pinch of salt; the same pinch that is required when investigating what we may consider great social changes, great transformations. Great transformations are never linear and firm; they may show, when compared, no uniformity. Even less are they unstoppable and historically necessitated; they are certainly less necessitated than the wisdom of hindsight may claim. Rather, they are the probable result of several causes that differ in their timing and their reach (Marx speaks, with misplaced redundancy, of over-determination). The timing in the interaction of prospective causes is of special significance. It makes a difference when (that is, at what point of its evolution and under what circumstances) a factor, trend or process converge (Pierson 2004). In fact, convergence does not fully reveal what is at play. The word may suggest the meeting of defined and self-contained factors, more than the merging of ongoing processes. It suggests simultaneity, but the word is imprecise when used to describe still evolving processes. Therefore, embracing terms such as social change or social transformation do not necessarily imply a sudden radical, decisive, indeed inescapable turn. This is even more so as evolving transformations are affected not only by factors and subjects that may, or intend to, foster them; they are also affected by resistance and opposition. They are further affected by the strategic collocation of the institutions that propel, resist or are otherwise caught in the process: their formal and factual powers, including the kind of veto powers that are a significant part of the American political system, and the timing of their engagement in the process. Despite all of this, a few transformations do reach a so-called point of no return, a point past which, as works on 'punctuated equilibria' and 'path dependence' (Krasner 1984) show, a series of initial choices tend to consolidate, thanks to the accumulation of positive feedback. Still, reaching a point of no return is rather a misnomer; a point of no return would, strictly speaking, put an end to history. The observation is important in regard to the evolution of the five presidential regimes Skowronek describes. They all consolidated, but they were and are not forever. So, if not for ever, then for how long? The question allows no firm answers, also because the construction of a replacing regime encounters all the vicissitudes, twists, and delays just illustrated. Granted, in sum, that for these

---

1.   Isaiah 21:12 'Watchman, what of the night? Watchman, what of the night? The watchman said, "The morning comes, and also the night. If you will inquire, inquire; return! Come back!"'

and other reasons, making predictions is not and should not be the task of the social scientist, I shall however close the chapter by responding to the analytical prudence suggested here with equally prudent, almost noncommittal expectations regarding the endurance of the neoliberal regime in the United States.

I stated in the closing pages of the last chapter that, following the 2008 election of Barak Obama, the Republican Party now in opposition followed an uncompromising strategy of resistance to Obama's presidential actions. This accounted for the policy constrictions Obama was saddled with. It equally accounted for why, in particular, his signature legislation, healthcare reform, was largely based on previous Republican ideas and proposals. Yet Republicans, even some who sponsored similar legislation when in office (Mitt Romney), vehemently opposed the bill and vehemently continue to oppose the implementation of what is now the law. They are managing to delay it by preventing or curtailing budgetary allocations and other measures needed for ongoing implementation. Of course, opposition to healthcare reform has a long history in the United States.[2] Resistance dates back to the beginning of the last century (Freddi 2012), and took roots with the diffusion, after the second postwar period, of tax-exempt private insurance, variably covered by employers and employees. Private insurance took over in opposition to President Truman's effort to socialise medicine. At first, labour unions resisted privatisation, but eventually they had to give up. In exchange they gained the right to negotiate aspects of its implementation. Other reform efforts, supported by presidents of both parties, followed, to little or no avail.

Still, opposition to 'Obamacare' reached documented levels of unique absurdity in its claims and allegations (Mann and Ornstein 2012). How was it possible? Was there no room for reason and conscience? Reason and conscience sound good and true. Who would question them? Their resonance continues to reflect a Gallic enlightenment conception of human reason, human choice, and human perfectibility. The conception assumes a number of self-congratulatory characteristics presiding over preferences and decisions. As summarised in George Lakoff's critical review of them, reason is supposedly conscious by definition; it adheres to facts; it is literal, abstract, dispassionate and universal (Lakoff 2008). Therefore, it does not need mediations. We reason with other people by way of language, and the language of reason does not interpret, does not influence, and does not need to vary. It is a supposedly objective tool, although perfectible by codification, for transmitting facts and data. Yet (Lakoff 2008: Ch.8) enlightenment concepts of reason and communication have little to do with reality and more to do with utopias and aspirations. I believe I have done my share in disabusing the reader on the role of language as a neutral, innocent tool of facts. I have been speaking of narratives in general as discourse, not as tested knowledge.

---

2. Resistance to implementation of major reforms, such as healthcare, may be particularly strong where implementation affects a whole string of established institutions and stakeholders. This might partially explain why Margaret Thatcher did not repeal the state's monopoly over England's *National Health Service*, and why the important health reforms proposed by the 2010 British Conservative Government preserve, albeit by decentralising it, the role of public institutions.

In the first chapter, I spoke of Locke's conception of civil society and its origins as a social naturalism narrative, presenting naturalism as an ontology, one that also happens to be morally superior to the artifice and arbitrariness of the state. I spoke of the way neoliberalism appropriated itself of that narrative, conveniently twisting it in the process. I spoke of problematisation and reproblematisation as a way of constructing or reconstructing realities otherwise left without meaning. And I spoke in this regard of the importance of *parrhesia*, of saying what we think, straight talking (*franc-parler*). *Parrhesia*, I specified, does not, however, mean speaking words that are inherently objective, always equal and universal. It does not assume that words pre-exist communication; that they are independent of their communicative role. Rather, it implies the opposite: that we seek a common language constructed by the *parrhesiastes*. Constructing a new, winning language is strategic during periods of intense political change, when the old order is contested and a new one is under construction. Speaking of the very few American presidents who repudiated an old regime and built a new one, Skowronek writes,

> [...] the presidency is not a place for complicated messages. The presidency's political interventions are too blunt and unsettling for a subtle and nuanced claim of legitimacy; the only irresistible appeal is the blunt, repudiative one. (Skowronek 2008: 95–96)

In times of turmoil, language tends to be simplified by the use of moral and emotional arguments, which may thus prevail. Simplification saves precious, constrained time. There are natural time limits as to how much information we can receive and organise. But this is not the most important reason for what Herbert Simon famously called 'bounded rationality'. We always simplify, to convince and be convinced. Even with ample time and even among decision makers, the unembellished language of facts and even more the tedious language of 'policy speak', the language of costs and benefits, the language of quantification, does not stick. We appreciate instead a language that gives us a sense of confidence in the new choices and the new conditions to which we are exposed. The more complex and stretched over time that the changes to which we are exposed are, the more difficult it is to shake off fears of unanticipated, possibly untoward consequences. We should not, therefore, be surprised if, given today's awareness of and aversion to risk, reforms intended to protect us from risk may not dispel but rather increase fears. It is in fact not surprising that 'Obamacare', a series of reforms intended to improve health coverage for present and prospective patients, may nonetheless meet with concern on the part of prospective beneficiaries. Presenting the reforms in the unadorned language of policy speak, as something that should simply stand to reason, may not easily dispel concerns. Uncertainty, concern, even rejection do not necessarily signal outright support for the neoliberal status quo. Rather, consumers' uncertainty and even resistance to Obamacare (in itself an effective, although reversible, sound bite) are reinforced by the fact that its implementation, even now that the law has been approved and the president has been re-elected, is staggered over a number of years. Hence, its outcomes (not just its outputs) remain uncertain. In the uncertainty, some consumers may prefer to keep the little they have rather than wait for what is promised but unclear as to its nature (Eckles and Schafter 2010). It is an established fact of social psychology that we attach greater value to what we fear to lose than to what we stand to gain. As to timing, as the saying goes, a bird in the hand is worth two in the bush. And if aversion to risk is paramount, we may prefer the present with all its costs to an imagined future where costs may prevail over uncertain benefits. To top it all, neoliberal opposition to Obamacare did a remarkable job of constructing and publicising a narrative of health reform that increased scepticism and fears in sectors of the electorate that were more sensitive to the potential personal costs of the reform.

In a context of uncertainties, like those above, the communicative role of would-be reformers is essential, as is the role of those who wish to justify their resistance to reform, as is the role of the mass media, whose job it should be to keep us informed. These are the communicators who crucially shape and condense reforms for public consumption; who package them as narratives supporting or opposing change. Framing (metaphors, images, formulae, representations, interpretations) and sound bites are among the tools employed to make the narratives easy and credible. With them, we construct and give meaning to the new realities associated with change and reforms. With them, we simplify by appealing to common sense and concreteness, intuition and emotions, memories and associations, the likely and the imaginable; with them, we simplify by individualising and bringing home the vivid effects of change. Narratives are intended to give reforms, or opposition to them, a quality of rightfulness that goes beyond *ratio*. By appealing to what is proper and right, they may even serve as a sort of *bildungsroman* for mass consumption. The role of communication has grown in importance with the information revolution, which embraces not only the spoken and written but also the visual message. And the latter has an influence and persuasion potential that, irrespective of its veracity, often goes beyond the former. But the craft of communication, the display of narratives and discourse, have an ancient ancestry, one that goes back, I surmise, to the passing of primitive communities, when facts and the way we see and judge them stopped coinciding. At that point, neither facts nor, for that matter, norms and understandings spoke for themselves. They needed a voice. At length, Rhetorics, the craft of arguing, was theorised and taught in the Magna Graecia and subsequently by Athenians and Romans. As a tool of persuasion for the operation of democratic and republican government, rhetorics went beyond unadorned, ostensibly neutral, documentation and demonstration.

When we then move to modernity, in which temporalities are compressed and making sense of ever new but possibly contingent realities is demanding, the active use of narratives for public persuasion becomes the norm. They become especially important when (not always positive) unanticipated changes occur. In many cases, narratives are condensed in powerful sound bites. *Muckraking* was the term famously used by Teddy Roosevelt to describe American investigative journalism's campaign, peaking during the Progressive Era, against the malfeasance of big monopoly corporations and the collusion between government and big business. The term ended up by defining and selling the progressive reforms Roosevelt pursued during his presidency. Today, the term defines a whole era. Other similarly condensing sound bites capturing defining aspects of specific nations are America's *Founding Fathers*, the *New Deal*, America's *melting pot*, the *American Dream*; nineteenth century unified Italy's *trasformismo*; German nineteenth century unification as *blut und boden* and *lebensraum*; and France as *civilisation* but Germany as *kultur.* Condensed narratives also abound in reference to colonial imperialism: France's *mission civilisatrice*; *the white man's burden*; British rule over India (*the jewel in the crown*) as the great British *Raj*; Orientalism. They abound as well when it comes to wars, victories and defeats (defeated World War I Germany's *stab in the back*, and Russia's victory in World War II as *The Great Patriotic War*). Also abundant are the narratives constructed by ethno-nationalist entrepreneurs to denounce the historical victimisation of their ethnicities at the hands of other ethnicities. Most significant, finally, are the narratives that Eric Hobsbawm (1983), in his treatment of Europe between the nineteenth and twentieth centuries, classified under *the invention of tradition* label.

Neoliberalism has done its own share of building powerful narratives and persuasive sound bites. Although neoliberal practices do not perfectly align with parties (the New Left's 'Third Way'), the main task of building neoliberal narratives, thus setting the terms of the debate defining the issues and drawing the boundaries of possible policies, has been carried out in the United States by the Republican Party (and in England by the Conservative successors of Margaret Thatcher). It has been carried out in the USA, since Ronald Reagan, irrespective of whether or not another Republican occupied the White House. If we compare nowadays the two dominant American parties in terms of their communicative skills, the Democrats, whether or not they control the presidency and other offices, no longer match the Republicans. They are largely compelled to address, defensively (*yes, but*), issues defined as materially and morally calamitous by the other side (a looming fiscal doomsday; the unsustainable financial costs of welfare entitlements; a culture of dependency; the excessive taxation of wealth creators; growing statism; the rapid erosion of individual liberties). As Somers and Block put it, '[...] when challenged by market fundamentalism, the impulse [of pragmatist opponents] to make concessions only serves to make [them] appear incoherent relative to the moral purity [of the former]' (Somers and Block 2005: 282). The reason for this condition of political subjection – a reason, not a tautology – is that the Democrats presently operate in a regime narrated, set up and still dominated by neoliberal true believers. And the ability to communicate, to construct a common language of persuasion, is the measure of a narrative that is still successfully supporting a long established regime. But supporting it for how much longer?

One factor in the endurance of the neoliberal regime in the Unites States has to do with its institutional checks and balances, and veto points. I could discuss the issue at greater length, but the essence of the argument is simple. Super-majorities are often needed to legislate and minorities can block policy making. Of this we have ample evidence under the presidency of Barak Obama. Still, this in itself does not explain the totally unprecedented and successful use of veto powers of all sorts during Obama's first term as president. Veto powers facilitated neoliberal resistance when it found itself in a numeric minority, but did not cause its tenacity and endurance. Resistance was a constant during all of Obama's first term: before the midterm elections of 2010, and with renewed energy and power after those elections and the rise of the Tea Party faction. There is no reason why attenuating some of the veto powers should significantly shorten neoliberalism's life or curb its self-assuredness.

The economist Michele Salvati foresaw American neoliberalism's endurance in two op-eds that appeared in the *Corriere della Sera*; the first on 9 September 2008, before the election of Obama, the second on 20 January 2009, the day Obama was inaugurated. In the first op-ed, Salvati considered the probable policy responses to the 2008 global recession. Probable responses, in themselves exceptional and dictated by exceptional circumstances, Salvati prognosticated, may temporarily curb the effects of adventurous neoliberal policies that, by deregulating a presumably self-correcting market, encouraged financial risk-taking and eventually opened the way to the fiscal collapse; but the responses will not suggest alternatives to the neoliberal model. Skowronek retrospectively concurs,

> [...] Obama seized the rhetoric of repudiation to press an expansive case for change. The problem with acting on this rhetoric, however, was that Obama also assumed the immediate burdens of crisis management [...] [The rhetoric] took a back seat to taxpayer support for corporations deemed 'too big to fail'. (Skowronek 2011: 179–180)

In effect, Obama picked up stabilisation policies that, pressed by the emergency, George W. Bush had set up before the end of his presidency. While time contingencies (the overlapping of the new presidency with the onset of the fiscal crisis) play a role in Skowronek's retrospective assessment of Obama's conduct, Salvati's prospective analysis is rooted in a broader view of historical changes and their contexts. In the past century, there have been, according to Salvati, two great turning points in the model of advanced capitalism: the advent of Keynesianism during the nineteen thirties and forties, followed in the nineteen seventies and eighties by the advent of neoliberalism. Their advent shared something that is at present absent. They shared the signs of a deep objective crisis in the previous model as well as (far more decisively in order to advance a new model), 'equally deep ideological, cultural, theoretical and finally political reorientations' (Salvati, M. *Corriere della Sera*, 20th Jan. 2009). The latter subjective features are today especially notable for their absence. I spoke above, with reservations, of reason and conscience as sufficient guides to decision making. I now add that, without those reorientations, the impersonal use of reason and documentation may not be sufficient to bring about those limited reforms that are dictated by and confined to the present emergency. If so, it should prove even more difficult to use the same reasonable language, stressing the reasons for the emergency, in order to push forward a regime generally alternative to and subversive of neoliberalism. Keynes stressed the importance of *animal spirits* as a stimulus to doing something new and positive. But if we are short of those spirits, emergencies may also keep in place constraints to what is possible, desirable and imaginable.

Salvati, from whom I borrow the title of this chapter, closed his first op-ed as follows,

> I remind those who prognosticate (or augur) radical changes [of] the answer Isaiah's watchman gave those who inquired how long the night would last: 'The morning will come, but it is still night; if you want to ask, come again'. (Salvati, 9 September 2008)

In his second op-ed of 20 January 2009, Salvati was still waiting for that morning, 'I believe it difficult that [Obama] will be able to chip away at the solid theoretical and ideological consensus that neoliberalism still enjoys'. As Obama moved toward the end of his first mandate, Skowronek, reflecting on what a second term would look like, seemed once more as prudent as Salvati in building scenarios for a second mandate. Pointing to the reconstructive job that would still await the president, he notes that, unlike Obama's presidency, previous reconstructive presidencies were able to pick up support from disillusioned partisan factions from the previous regime. Previous reconstructive presidencies were all characterised by the emergence of new interest coalitions, new institutional instruments and new power configurations. This has not been the case for the Obama presidency. Without them, even legislative successes may not upset the politics of the past. Obamacare offers a good example. The passage of the health reform in April 2010 owed much to Obama's ability '[...] to weave a major reform through the tickets of interests that controlled things as he found them [...] [B]ut does action like that transform American politics?' (Skowronek 2011: 186).

The Skowronek scenario[3] that I personally find most intriguing, and most convincing in suggesting the reason for the neoliberal endurance points to the fact that, contrary to other transformative regimes, the one inaugurated by Ronald Reagan has not yet finished, as of today, its transformative job of dismantling the institutional and programmatic inheritance of the previous, New Deal regime. This is so, despite the fact that neoliberalism has proved strong in its narrative, strong in affecting partisan and interest realignments, and strong, I would add, in the active employment of the tools of governing at a distance. The main reason of the unfinished job is that the long New Deal left behind a state transformed and enriched like no other before by its policies, programmes and institutions of social transformation. It left behind the state actively governing with society which I described in my early chapters. Skowronek comments:

> With so much of the infrastructure of liberalism and progressivism still in place, [...] movement conservatives have never been at a loss for targets to mobilise against [...] Their reconstructive rhetoric continues to resonate with a clarity and simplicity no longer matched on the America left. (Skowronek 2011: 189)[4]

---

3. Skowronek is more guarded in drawing conclusions.

4. Skowronek and other analysts use the terms 'conservative' and similar ('neoconservative', 'social conservative') while I and others use the term 'neoliberal'. The latter is a term used by the scholarly originators of neoliberalism, and later by its critics. It is meant to convey the unique intellectual and political meaning of the neoliberal movement as one purported to pursue a return to the essence of liberalism as autonomy and individualism.

The quote nicely captures neoliberalism's escalating activism and confrontational ideology since the beginning of the new century. It may be true that that increasingly adversarial stance has been mostly marked by unheard-of vetoes, obstructionisms and repeated forays (a kind of trench warfare); and these strategies, by endangering the every-day operation of governing institutions, may at long last break up the neoliberal coalition (of which break-up, however, there are hardly any signs) and marginalise the movement. Meanwhile, in the latest and biggest game of chicken between Mr. Obama and the Republican Party – that involving the so-called sequester – the Republican Party, despite general expectations, did not flinch at the purposely Solomonic nature of the presidentially threatened across-the-board cuts (1 March 2013). The President lost and neoliberals moved a step closer to starving the beast. Eighty-five billions of additional budget cuts may be a pittance, as neoliberals say, for a budget of a few trillions. But it is not a pittance for the common people – including, most likely, the women and men that serve in the military – who will end up bearing the brunt of the sacrifices.

Nonetheless, these are current events, the long-term outcomes of which social scientists cannot predict ('It is still night'). Whatever the outcome, these events confirm the fact that the ongoing contest is, if I may be platitudinous, a contest for the American soul. Better said, they add to the evidence that neoliberalism, especially in the United States but also in other advanced democracies (and conspicuously in international economic organisations), is not another variation on the theme of democratic liberalism, but a movement subversive of what the democratic state (in the acquitting of collective responsibilities and in its close relations with civil society and its public sphere) has been all along.

It is not irrelevant, in terms of neoliberalism's middle-range future that, if a world hegemon still exists, it is the Unites States. Nor is it of indifference that China, an authoritarian regime competing for hegemony, has also embarked (since the end of the seventies) on a converging model of development with clear neoliberal features.

Still, if you wish to ask, ask me later. Will it help? Later, I might still be forced to retrench behind Polanyi's prophecy,

> Our thesis is that the idea of a self-adjusting market implied a stark utopia. Such an institution could not exist for any length of time without annihilating the human and natural substance of society; it would have physically destroyed man and transformed his surroundings into a wilderness. (Polanyi 1957: 3)

This is a prophecy indeed, but a prophecy of what? Is it a prophecy of social disintegration or of a newly embedded liberalism?

Bibliography

Akerlof, G. and Shiller, R. (2009) *Animal Spirits: How human psychology drives the economy, and why it matters for global capitalism*, Princeton: Princeton University Press.

Alexander, M. (2010) *The New Jim Crow: Mass incarceration in the age of colorblindness*, New York: The New Press.

Arendt, H. (1958) *The Origins of Totalitarianism*, New York: Meridian Books.

Barry, J., Osborne, T. and Rose, N. (eds) (1996) *Foucault and Political Reason: Liberalism, neoliberalism and rationalities of government*, Chicago: Chicago University Press.

Beck, U. (1992) *Risk Society: Toward a New Modernity*, London: Sage Publications.

— (1998) *Democracy without Enemies*, Cambridge: Polity Press.

— (1999) *World Risk Society*, Cambridge: Polity Press.

— (2000) *The Brave New World of Work*, Cambridge: Polity Press.

— (2009) *World at Risk,* Cambridge: Polity Press.

Blyth, M. (2002) *Great Transformations: Economic ideas and institutional change in the Twentieth Century*, Cambridge: Cambridge University Press.

Bourdieu, P. (1998) *Acts of Resistance Against the Tyranny of the Market*, New York: New Press.

Bozovic, M. (ed.) (1995) *The Panopticon Writings,* London: Verso.

Brown, W. (2003) 'Neoliberalism and the end of liberal democracy', *Theory and Event*, 7(1): 1–36.

— (2006) 'American nightmare: neoliberalism, neoconservatism, and de-democratization', *Political Theory*, 34(6): 690–714.

Castel, R. (1991) 'From Dangerousness to Risk', in G. Burchell, C. Gordon and P. Miller (eds) *The Foucault Effect: Studies in governmentality*, Chicago: Chicago University Press, pp. 281–98.

Ceri, P. (2003) *La società vulnerabile. Quale sicurezza, quale libertà*, Bari: Laterza.

Dean, M. (1999a) *Governamentality: Power and rule in modern society*, London: Sage Publications.

— (1999b) 'Normalizing Democracy: Foucault and Habermas on democracy, liberalism and law', in S. Ashenden and D. Owen (eds), *Foucault contra Habermas*, London: Sage, pp. 166–94.

Diamond, L. and Morlino, L. (2004) 'The quality of democracy', *CDDRL Working Papers*, 20, pp.1–35.

Di Palma, G. (1977) *Surviving without Governing: The Italian parties in parliament*, Berkeley and Los Angeles: University of California Press.

Douglas, M. (1992) *Risk and Blame: Essays in cultural theory*, London and New York: Routledge.

Douglas, M. and Wildavsky, A. (1982) *Risk and Culture*, Berkeley and Los Angeles: University of California Press.

Dumont, L. (1970) *Homo Hierarchicus: The cast system and its implications*, London: Weidenfeld & Nicolson.

Eckles, D. L. and Schaffner, B. F. (2010) 'Loss aversion and the framing of the health care debate', *The Forum*, 8(1) Article 7.

Elias, N. (1969, 1982) *The Civilizing Process*, Vol. I., *The History of Manners*, Vol. II, *State Formation and Civilization*, Oxford: Blackwell.

Evans, P., Rueschemeyer, D. and Skocpol, T. (eds) (1985) *Bringing the State Back In*, Cambridge: Cambridge University Press.

Ferrera, M. (2005) *The Boundaries of Welfare*, New York: Oxford University Press.

Foucault, M. (1975) *Surveiller et punir*, Paris: Gallimard.

—   (1977) *Discipline and Punish*, New York: Vintage Books.

—   (1982) 'The Subject and Power', in H. L. Dreyfus and P. Rabinow, *Michel Foucault: Beyond structuralism and hermeneutics*, Chicago: University of Chicago Press, pp. 208–26.

—   (1988) 'Social Security', in L. Kritzman (ed.) *Michel Foucault, Politics, Philosophy, Culture: Interviews and other writings (1977–1984)*, New York: Routledge, pp. 159–77.

—   (1991a) 'Questions of Method', in G. Burchell, C. Gordon and P. Miller (eds) *The Foucault Effect: Studies in governmentality*, Chicago: Chicago University Press, pp. 73–86.

—   (1991b) 'Governmentality', in G. Burchell, C. Gordon and P. Miller (eds) *The Foucault Effect: Studies in governmentality*, Chicago: Chicago University Press, pp. 87–104.

—   (2008) *The Birth of Biopolitics*, New York: Palgrave Macmillan.

Fraser, N. (1981) 'Foucault on modern power: empirical insights and normative confusions', *Praxis International*, 1(3): 272–87.

Freddi, S. G. (1989) 'Burocrazia, democrazia e governabilità', in G. Freddi (a cura di), *Scienza dell'amministrazione e politiche pubbliche*, Roma: La Nuova Italia Scientifica, pp. 19–65.

—   (2012) *L'anomalia americana. Perché è tanto difficile, se non impossibile, riformare la sanità statunitense*, Milano: Vita e Pensiero.

Friedman, L. (2002) *The Horizontal Society*, New Haven: Yale University Press.

Friedrichs, J. (2010) 'The Privatization of Force and its Consequences: Unintended but not unpredictable', in C. Daase and C. Friesendorf (eds) *Rethinking Security Governance: The problem of unintended consequences*, London and New York: Routledge, pp. 176–97.

Garapon, A. (2012) *Lo stato minimo. Il neoliberalismo e la giustizia*, Milano: Raffaello Cortina Editore.

Garland, D. (2001) *The Culture of Control: Crime and social order in contemporary society*, Chicago: University of Chicago Press.

Giddens, A. (1998) *The Third Way: The renewal of social democracy*, Cambridge: Polity Press.

—   (2000) *The Third Way and Its Critics*, London: Polity Press.

Ginsburg, T. and Moustafa, T. (eds) (2008) *Rule by Law: The politics of courts in authoritarian regimes*, New York: Cambridge University Press.

Gordon, C. (1991) 'Government Rationality: An introduction', in G. Burchell, C. Gordon and P. Miller (eds) *The Foucault Effect: Studies in governmentality*, Chicago: Chicago University Press, pp. 1–51.

Gorski, P. (2003) *The Disciplinary Revolution: Calvinism and the rise of the state in early modern Europe*, Chicago: University of Chicago Press.

Gosselin, P. (2008) *High Wire: The precarious financial lives of American families*, New York: Basic Books.

Greenhouse, S. (2008) *The Big Squeeze: Tough times for the American worker*, New York: Knopf.

Habermas, J. (1991) The Structural Transformation of the Public Sphere, Cambridge, Mass.: MIT Press.

Hacker, J., Mettler, S. and Soss, J. (2007) 'The New Politics of Inequality: A policy-centered perspective', in J. Soss, J. Hacker and S. Mettler (eds) Remaking America: Democracy and public policy in an age of inequality, New York: Russell Sage, pp. 3–23.

Hayek, F. (1944) The Road to Serfdom, Chicago: University of Chicago Press.

Harrison, B. (1994) Lean and Mean: Why large corporations will continue to dominate the global economy, New York: Guilford Press.

Harvey, D. (2005) A Brief History of Neoliberalism, Oxford: Oxford University Press.

Hibou, B. (2012) La bureaucratisation du monde à l'ère néolibérale, Paris: La Découverte.

Hirschman, A. (1970) Exit, Voice, and Loyalty: Responses to decline in firms, organizations, and states, Cambridge, Mass.: Harvard University Press.

—   (1991) *The Rhetoric of Reaction: Perversity, futility, jeopardy*, Cambridge, Mass.: The Belknap Press of Harvard University Press.

Hobsbawm, E. and Ranger, T. (eds) (1983) *The Invention of Tradition*, Cambridge: Cambridge University Press.

Holden, A. and Shuler, K. (2013) *Beyond the Bars: A new model of 'virtual incarceration' for low-risk offenders*, Deloitte Consulting, Westlake, Texas: Deloitte University Press.

Holmes, S. and Sunstein, C. (1999) *The Cost of Rights: Why liberty depends on taxes*, New York: W. W. Norton & Company.

Jacobs, L. and Skocpol, T. (eds) (2005) *Inequality and American Democracy: What we know and what we need to learn*, New York: Russell Sage.

Jobert, B. (ed.) (1994) *Le tournant néo-libéral en Europe*, Paris: Éditions L'Harmattan.

Jonas, H. (1973) 'Technology and responsibility: reflections on the new tasks of ethics', *Social Research*, 15(2): 1–15.

Keynes, J. M. (1936) *The General Theory of Employment, Interest and Money*, London: Macmillan.

Koselleck, R. (2002) *The Practice of Conceptual History: Timing history, spacing concepts*, Stanford: Stanford University Press.

Krasner, S. (1984) 'Approaches to the state: alternative conceptions and historical dynamics', *Comparative Politics*, 16(2): 223–46.

Kornhauser, W. (1959) *The Politics of Mass Society*, Glencoe, Ill.: The Free Press.

Kritzman, L. (ed.) (1988) *Foucault: Politics, philosophy, culture: interviews and other writings, 1977–84*, New York: Routledge.

Krugman, P. (2012) *End this Depression Now*, New York: Norton.

Kuran, T. (1995) *Private Truths, Public Lies: The social consequences of preference falsification*, Cambridge, Mass.: Harvard University Press.

Lakoff, G. (2008) *The Political Mind*, New York: Viking.

Landau, M. (1969) '*Redundancy*, rationality, and the problem of duplication and overlap', *Public Administration Review* 29(4): 346–58.

Lilla, M. (2007) *The Stillborn God: Religion, politics, and the modern west*, New York: Knopf.

Lippmann, W. (1922) *Public Opinion*, New York: Harcourt, Brace and Co.

Lipset, S. M. (1960) *Political Man*, Garden City, NY: Doubleday.

Luhmann, N. (1993) *Risk: A sociological theory*, New York: de Gruyter.

Lyon, D. (1994) *The Electronic Eye: The rise of surveillance society*, Minneapolis: University of Minnesota Press.

Madrick, J. (2009) *The Case for Big Government*, Princeton: Princeton University Press.

Mann, T. and Ornstein, N. (2012) *Even Worse than It Looks: How the American constitutional system collided with the new politics of extremism*, New York: Basic Books.

Manzoni, A. (1909 [1825]) *I promessi sposi*, New York: P. F. Collier and Son.

March, J. and Olsen, J. (1995) *Democratic Governance*, New York: The Free Press.

Marshall, T. H. (1964) *Class, Citizenship and Social Development*, New York: Doubleday.

Marx, K. (1970 [1843]) *Critique of Hegel's Philosophy of Right* in J. O'Malley (ed.) *Marx's Critique of Hegel's Philosophy of Right*, Cambridge, CUP.

Mencher, S. (1967) *Poor Law to Poverty Program: Economic security policy in Britain and the United States*, Pittsburgh: University of Pittsburgh Press.

Mirowski, P. (2010) 'The great mortification: economists' responses to the crisis of 2007-(and Counting)', *Hedgehog Review* 12(2).

Mirowski, P. and Plehwe, D. (eds) (2009) *The Road from Mont Pélerin: The making of the neoliberal thought collective*, Cambridge, Mass.: Harvard University Press.

Morozov, E. (2013) *To Save Everything Click Here*, New York: Public Affairs.

Murphy, L. and Nagel, T. (2002) *The Myth of Ownership: Taxes and justice*, Oxford: Oxford University Press.

Paxton, R. (2013) 'Vichy lives! – in a way', *New York Review of Books*, April 2013: 21.

Pellicani, L. (2010) *Anatomia dell'anticapitalismo*, Soveria Mannelli: Rubbettino.

Pierson, P. (2004) *Politics in Time*, Princeton: Princeton University Press.

Poggi, G. (1990) *The State, Its Nature, Development and Prospects*, Stanford: Stanford University Press.

Polanyi, K. (1957 [1944]) *The Great Transformation*, Boston: Beacon Press.

Pollan, M. (2002) *The Botany of Desire*, New York: Random House.

Przeworski, A. (1986) 'Some Problems in the Study of the Transition to Democracy', in G. O'Donnell, P. Schmitter and L. Whitehead (eds) *Transitions from Authoritarian Rule: Comparative perspectives*, Baltimore: The Johns Hopkins University Press, pp. 47–63.

Putnam, R. (1995) 'Bowling alone: America's declining social capital', *Journal of Democracy* 6(1): 65–78.

Rich, M. (2013) 'Should we make crime impossible?', *Harvard Journal of Law and Public Policy* 36(2): 795–846.

Rose, N. (1996) 'Governing "Advanced" Liberal Democracies', in A. Barry, T. Osborne and N. Rose (eds) *Foucault and Political Reason*, Chicago: Chicago University Press.

Ruggie, J. (1982) 'International regimes, transactions, and change: embedded liberalism in the postwar economic order', *International Organization* 36: 379–415.

Sandel, M. (2012) *What Monet Can't Buy: The moral limits of markets*, New York: Farrar, Straus and Giroux.

Sartori, G. (1987) *The Theory of Democracy Revisited*, Chatam, N.J.: Chatam House.

Schlesinger, M. (2005) 'The Dangers of the Market Panacea', in J. Morone and L. Jacob (eds) (2005) *Healthy, Wealthy, & Fair: Health care and the good society*, New York: Oxford University Press, pp. 91–132.

Self, P. (1993) *Government by the Market? The politics of public choice*, Boulder & San Francisco: Westview Press.

Sennett, R. (1998) *The Corrosion of Character: The personal consequences of work in the new capitalism*, New York: Norton.

Skocpol, T. (1992) *Protecting Soldiers and Mothers: The political origins of social policy in the United States*, Cambridge, Mass.: Belknap Press of Harvard University Press.

Skowronek, S. (1993 [1997] 2nd edn) *The Politics Presidents Make*, Cambridge, Mass.: Belknap Press of Harvard University Press.

—— (2008 [2011] 2nd edn) *Presidential Leadership in Political Time*, Lawrence Kansas: University of Kansas Press.

Smith, H. (2012) *Who Stole the American Dream?*, New York: Random House.

Somers, M. (2008) *Genealogies of Citizenship: Markets, statelessness, and the right to have rights*, New York: Cambridge University Press.

Somers, M. and Block, F. (2005) 'From poverty to perversity: ideas, markets, and institutions over 200 years of welfare debate', *American Sociological Review* 70(2): 260–87.

Soss, J., Hacker, J. and Mettler, S. (eds) (2007) *Remaking America: Democracy and public policy in an age of inequality*, New York: Russell Sage.

Stiglitz, J. E. (2012) *The Price of Inequality: How today's divided society endangers our future*, New York: Norton.

Strydom, P. (2002) *Risk, Environment and Society*, Philadelphia: Open University Press.

Stuntz, W. (2011) *The Collapse of American Criminal Justice*, Cambridge, Mass.: The Belknap Press of Harvard University Press.

Suleiman, E. (2003) *Dismantling Democratic States*, Princeton: Princeton University Press.

Sunstein, C. (2005) *Laws of Fear: Beyond the precautionary principle*, New York: Cambridge University Press.

Thaler, R. and Sunstein, C. (2008) *Nudge: Improving decisions about health, wealth, and happiness*, New Haven: Yale University Press.

Thatcher, M. (1993) *The Downing Street Years*, London: HarperCollins.

Tocqueville, A. de (1994 [1840]) *Democracy in America*, Part 2, Book II, New York: Everyman's Library.

Verkuil, P. (2007) *Outsourcing Sovereignty*, New York: Cambridge University Press.

Vogel, D. (2012) *The Politics of Precaution: Regulating health, safety, and environmental risks in Europe and the United States*, Princeton: Princeton University Press.

Weber, M. (1958) 'Bureaucracy', in H. H. Gerth and C. W. Mills (eds) *From Max Weber: Essays in Sociology*, New York: Oxford University Press, pp. 196–244.

Winters, J. (2011) 'Oligarchy and democracy', *The American Interest*, 7(2): 1–13.

Wulf, H. (2007) 'Challenging the Weberian concept of the state: the future of the monopoly of violence', *The Australian Center for Peace and Conflict Studies* Occasional Papers Series, 9.

Young, J. (1999) *The Exclusive Society: Social exclusion, crime and difference in late modernity*, London: Sage Publications.

— (2007) *The Vertigo of Late Modernity*, London: Sage Publications.

Zweig, J. (2007) *Your Money and Your Brain*, New York: Simon and Schuster.

Index

Lightning Source UK Ltd.
Milton Keynes UK
UKOW04f1835191113

221435UK00002B/11/P